FROM OUT OF THE FIRESTORM

A Memoir of the Holocaust

FROM OUT OF THE FIRESTORM

A Memoir of the Holocaust

by Rachela and Sam Walshaw

SHAPOLSKY PUBLISHERS
NEW YORK

This book is dedicated to those whom I shall never forget:

My dear grandparents, dearest Mother and Father, beloved sister and brothers, uncles, aunts, cousins and friends. Until my final breath, this book, this life, is a monument to your memory.

CONTENTS

ACKNOWLEDGMENTS

My special gratitude to my brother and sister-in-law, Sam and Elaine Walshaw. Without their kind support this book could not have existed.

I owe much to my husband, Herbert, who patiently heard my accounts and gave me the courage to put them down on paper. My thanks go out as well to fellow Hadassah members Shirley Aurback and Jennie Ritzner, who encouraged me to turn my scattered memoirs into a book-length manuscript.

My sons, Solomon and Joseph, helped shape the emerging drafts of this gift to them and their generation, while author Isaac Kowalski was a valuable guide to the publishing world.

From that point my gratitude goes to the staff of Shapolsky Publishers and, specifically, to the friendly and skillful editorial services of Isaac Mozeson.

FOREWORD

I was among the crowd when Professor Shimon Dubnow, the renowned Jewish historian, visited Vilna in 1939 before the outbreak of the war. Thousands of Jews had come from the city to the railroad station to greet him. We formed a great procession that escorted him to his quarters.

Only two years later he would perish in the Riga Ghetto. In December of 1941, just before he was killed, his voice rang out with an unforgettable cry: *"Shreibt un farshiebt!"* (write and record — bear witness).

I was assigned by the United Partisan Organization to the former YIVO building, where Jews were given forced labor. We were secretly stockpiling arms and munitions smuggled in from our contacts on the outside.

The German occupation forces used this same building to hoard the Jewish cultural treasures they plundered. A group of "experts" from the staff of Alfred von Rosenberg were collecting Jewish memorabilia from all over Eastern Europe to be shipped to a storage facility in Frankfurt-am-Main, Germany. The ultimate goal was a museum of the extinct European Jew.

Among our special work detail was the linguist and historian Zelig Kalmanowitch. He was appointed by the Germans to write up the history of the Karaites. This historian met his end in a concentration camp in Estonia in 1944. Before his deportation, Kalmanowitch charged me and my colleagues to record everything for the benefit of future generations.

As a former partisan, I consider it a sacred duty to fulfill the requests of Dubnow, Kalmanowitch and millions of their fellow victims. It is a special task to present this brief foreword to the memoirs of Rachela Walshaw Schlufman. The manuscript I read richly deserved to be published, and it is my privilege to help get *FROM OUT OF THE FIRESTORM* to the widest possible audience.

Why add yet another holocaust memoir to the formidable list of similar books? There is no duplication in these accounts. Each record is a precious tile in the whole mosaic, filling in more details, impressions, names and lives. Rachela's vivid and expressive book contains some especially unique experiences, and the lay reader and the historian both are grateful for her miraculous survival and the strength of her articulate testimony. Her brother Sam's story is also remarkable; I learned much about the life of young survivors who were brought to England.

I congratulate Rachela and Sam for this important achievement, and I sincerely recommend that the public avail themselves of this valuable publication.

Isaac Kowalski
Author of *A Secret Press in Nazi Europe* and editor of the four-volume *Anthology on Armed Jewish Resistance 1939-1945*.
New York, 1990

INTRODUCTION

The history of the world has been a series of small holocausts. If we forget the unprecented Nazi atrocities of our era, the future will blaze with holocausts as well.

No great city walls of civilization, no tall museums of culture can stay the march of death and destruction by genocidal hatred. Our only defenses, our only means of salvation are the edifices of memory. If we remember the glow from the cremetoria, we can perhaps remember that the pink of sunrise should promise beauty and hope for all people of all races, religions and nations. Only as sisters and brothers of memory can we band together to crush the head of future holocausts.

This memory must not merely be a cherished ideal. The Holocaust was idealism, Romanticism gone mad. Holocausts can only be fought with the realistic idealism of memory. Every book, every tape, every film, every artifact on the Holocaust is a hedge against future destruction.

With the force of a firestorm the German army swept over Poland in September of 1939. Many cities, including our little town of Wonchok, were burned and gutted. By the time the smoke cleared, hundreds of thousands of Jews in and around my hometown had vanished in the furnaces of Treblinka.

My memories only awaken during sleepless nights. That is when I think about my youth, my home, my family. I then roam every corner of the little houses where my friends and neighbors lived. I can still hear their voices and bits of gossip that twittered from neighbor to neighbor. It is painful to think about the fate of all those lives and all that culture which has long since vanished. Today there are only dreams left . . . and the narratives of some survivors. It is these accounts that have best survived the Holocaust.

I

The Stolen Wedding

Memory is a peculiar editor. Most of life is left on the cutting room floor. The remaining memories, both sad and beautiful, are mixed together for us to pick out and make comprehensible. Sometimes that is impossible.

One of my earliest and most vivid memories is of my eldest sister's wedding in 1931. Tobcia was seventeen years old when she and Seharie married in grand Hasidic style. I was seven, just starting public school and feeling very grown up at the time. The event unfolded before my eyes like a fairy tale.

Seharie was twelve years older than my sister, a man of twenty-nine who was well-established as a lumber dealer. Tobcia proudly displayed her bridal finery to all her friends, as I looked on in awe of all the beautiful lace and jewelry that were such lustrous strangers in our workaday home. Relatives from all over Poland were expected, and preparation for the gathering started early. A woman was hired to do all the cooking and baking. She spent a great deal of her time chasing me out of the kitchen, complaining that my friends and I were disturbing her. I resented being excluded, but there was no arguing with her. She wore a black dress, a black apron, and her head was wrapped in a white turban. She was a conscientious worker and had an excellent reputation as a cook. With each new creation, my parents complimented her talents.

Dishes and tablecloths were rented for the wedding. The baker donated his oven to us for the day in order to roast all the chickens, ducks and geese, as well as to bake the amazing array of pastries.

Soon everyone in the family was brought in to lend a hand. "What can you do?" my mother asked when I volunteered my services. I insisted that I was perfectly capable of cleaning the soda glasses and make them sparkle. "Here," Mother said as she handed me a piece of cloth. "Do your job well and it will be a Mitzvah for us all."

I wiped each glass carefully as I removed it from its carton. I was brimming with confidence to have been entrusted with this task. But I must have performed my job a little too zealously because before I knew it one of the glasses had broken in my hand and I fainted from the pain. My mother nearly fainted, as well, from the sight of all the blood, but she managed to call a neighbor for help. The bleeding stopped, but I was distraught that I would have to go to the wedding wearing a big linen bandage.

My mother had a beautiful red silk dress made for me. A new pair of patent leather shoes, quite an extravagance in those days, also helped me to forget about my bandaged hand.

With the wedding day's approach, everyone pitched in to help move the furniture into the backyard to make room for the rented tables and chairs. That is when I began to feel that it was all really happening.

The celebration commenced on Thursday night and lasted through Sunday. Tobcia's friends arrived early to help my mother set up and to help dress the bride. Tobcia was a pretty girl with blond hair, blue eyes, high cheekbones and a slender figure. She was stunning in her pure white gown and her pearl inlaid veil. I stared in amazement at my sister. She had been transformed into a queen.

Soon the entertainment arrived. This consisted of a gentleman wearing a long black suit and two violin players. My mother immediately fed them to give them the strength to play through the entire celebration. Mother then sent the cook off to the bakery to check on the food. This was the first of her children to be married off, and she was determined that everything go perfectly.

By the time evening fell, guests of all ages started to flow into the house. The sun had set, and the chupa, the marriage canopy, gleamed against the night sky as it was put into place in the middle of the courtyard. Four young boys held the corner poles of the canopy.

Suddenly, the lovely sounds of Hebrew melodies, clapping hands and dancing could be heard filtering into the house. The groom, flanked by his father and mine, made his dramatic entrance. Tobcia met them, and the men gathered around as Seharie lifted her veil and gazed upon her radiant face. Ever since biblical Jacob, this ritual ensured that the chosen bride was indeed the woman beneath the veil.

I was beside myself with excitement, running back and forth from the house to the courtyard. I wanted to see everything, but I was too little to see over the heads of the adults. Seharie stood under the chupa awaiting his bride-to-be. Finally, the magical moment came. Tobcia was escorted through the waves of hovering guests by the two mothers. My mother held a long lit candle. Tobcia wore a white satin kerchief over the veil which again covered her face. Minutes later, the crunching of crystal underfoot was followed by a barrage of firecrackers. A resounding "mazel tov" was heard almost as loud.

It was time for the food. The bountiful tables were covered with brocaded linens; there were pastries and drinks everywhere. Gallons of beer flowed.

I looked all around but could see none of my family in the crowd. Then I heard a commotion in the kitchen and went there to find my mother in tears and my grandmother patting cold water on her face. The cook, too, holding a handkerchief to her nose, was crying. I couldn't imagine what was going on, but I was frightened to see my mother in such a state. I ran to find my father and soon most of the family had gathered in the kitchen to hear bad news.

While Moshe the baker and his wife were enjoying my sister's wedding, some Poles had broken into the bakery and stolen the main course which was cooking in the oven. In the midst of this crisis, everyone forgot about Tobcia who was nowhere to be seen. I found the bride up in her bedroom weeping over her misfortune. I fell at her long hair and cried with her.

Eventually we both came downstairs and were surprised to see the guests carrying on with their drinking and dancing as if nothing had happened.

For those thieves, our roasting birds were more dear than diamonds, but our family and friends had proved themselves even more valuable by maintaining their joyous celebration in the face of this disaster.

By the time the guests had said their farewells, the house had been emptied of all the rented tables and chairs. Our dear grandparents had taken their leave and order had been restored to our home. Eventually, the story of Tobcia's nuptial thieves could be shared with some humor. Now, however, when I recall Tobcia's wedding, the stolen feast seems to hover over the event like a dark cloud. The gentiles would go on to far more serious plunder.

II

The World of Wonchok

The years rose and fell around us. We were a family of ten, five brothers and three sisters whose lives intertwined with parents, grandparents, aunts, uncles, cousins, friends, neighbors and schoolmates. The town of Wonchok was the world to me then, an uneventful precious little world. My parents sometimes spoke of the horrors of the first World War, but our little community seemed safe from hunger and disease. It seemed as if nothing could go wrong. Still my father prayed that his children would never be visited by the nightmare of war.

Being religious, prayer was a central part of our lives. My father and brothers spent much of their time at the shul immersed in prayer, study and Talmudic debate. The community was clearly divided between Poles and Jews. There were about five hundred Polish families and only about one hundred Jewish ones, but we all lived and worked in relative peace. There were no ghettos then. Jews could live anywhere in town, but generally chose to live together. It made sense. After all, what Jewish parents would not want their children to grow up safely and securely among their own kind?

Though I went to school with Christians, my knowledge of the private workings of the Christian world was limited. The Catholic priests who ran our school were strict but fair and excused us from participating in their prayers. On the whole, my gentile classmates were a decent lot with whom we remained distant but friendly. We were not invited to their homes ;nor were they invited to ours.

Our landlord was a pious Catholic who had grown up in America. After making his fortune there, he returned to his homeland to find himself a proper wife. He intended to bring his bride back to the States with him, but when his father fell ill, he decided to remain in Poland. He bought and managed our house and periodically delighted us with stories of America. He found his "proper" wife and built her a house in back of ours.

All this changed our lives. We children were used to having the run of the yard. Suddenly, it was off limits to us. Our landlord's bride was from a prestigious family, and she found it beneath her dignity to live in such small quarters — behind Jews, no less. In short time she succeeded in turning her husband into an Old World Polish anti-Semite like herself.

For the first time we could not build our own Sukkah during the Festival of Booths. This was terribly disappointing. It forced us to carry our meals to a neighbor's sukkah for the week.

Our landlord's wife soon became pregnant, but our landlord never lived to see his child. The victim of a sudden heart attack, he was dressed up in a black wedding suit and hastily laid out in a mahogany casket. Four tall candlesticks burnt steadily around him. The young widow went back to live with her parents and left her husband's body unattended for three days.

My father, being a cohen, could not stay in such close proximity to the dead body, so he ate and slept at the shul. Left to my own devices, I felt myself drawn to the window of the little house. The room was clouded over with smoke from the candles. The smell of incense filled the air. Finally, he was taken away to be buried. It was my first brush with the mysterious ways of the other world that surrounded me. This specter of death was unsettling. I felt sad for the baby who would be born without a father, and I was struck by the loneliness of this ritual. How different it was from the community oriented customs of the Jews.

But I was too busy to dwell on the fate of our poor landlord. Every day after public school I attended a girls' Hebrew school. I loved the Hebrew lessons and folk dancing, and I would delight my father with newly acquired tales from Jewish history.

My childhood was filled with stories, most of them exchanged on Shabbos when all work stopped and my parents could relax from their busy week. With each story I learned more about my family. One of my favorites, that my father would tell, was about how I came to be named. My grandparents, Jerome and Rachel Walshaw lived on Kolojova Street in Skarzysko, Poland, close to the railroad station. Theirs was a busy street filled with many stores, boarding houses and restaurants. Travelers found it convenient to shop there or spend the night in one of the local rooming houses.

My grandparents owned one of the best Kosher restaurants in the area. Grandma Rachel ran an efficient business and had a great personality for working with people. She was also quite an expert in the kitchen, and it was not unusual for her to instruct the cook on how to prepare meals for particular clients. Her restaurant became famous and people from all over came to Kolojova to dine.

But Rachel was not only a businesswoman; she was also a wife and mother. Jerome, her husband, was a sweet, knowledgeable man who had spent most of his life studying Talmud and Jewish law. Because he was adept in conversation he was also a big asset to the business.

Rachel was always surrounded by people. Even on Shabbos, the day of rest, she found pleasure in inviting friends to her home. One couple, in particular, Jacob and Rivka Teitelbaum, was extremely close to Rachel and Jerome.

Rachel and Rivka had been childhood friends. Even marriage had not interrupted their friendship, and, by coincidence, both women became pregnant at the same time.

In the months ahead, however, Jacob and Rivka left Skarzysko to settle in a city called Radoszyce. Rachel was heart-broken, but the two best friends wrote to each other regularly.

In December of 1894, Rachel wrote to Rivka with news of the birth of her son Shlomo. Rivka was very happy and soon had her own good news. She had given birth to a lovely girl named Baila. With God's help their long-range plans to be in-laws was now underway. They both hoped that the future would bring marital happiness to their two children.

Over the next several years the two women had little time to keep up their correspondence. Both Rachel and Rivka were busy giving birth and raising families. Soon Rachel had six children and Rivka had five. Both families were blessed in that all the children were healthy and bright.

Seventeen years passed before Jacob and Rivka could take a trip to Skarzysko. The first thing they did when they reached their home town — even before seeing their own families — was to call on Rachel and Jerome. The reunion was a happy one filled with amazement over the swift passage of time.

Jacob and Rivka were particularly impressed by Rachel's eldest son Shlomo. He was good-looking, tall and slim, with all the qualifications necessary to be chosen for their Baila.

When the right time came, Jacob and Rivka approached their friends. Normally a shadkhin arranged marriages, but this was a special case. The happy mothers embraced each other remembering with joy their long-held hope of joining families.

The distant future had arrived. Rivka spoke of Baila's merits, commenting on how beautiful, kind and sweet she was. Shlomo needed little convincing before agreeing to take Baila as his bride-to-be.

A happy Rachel busily prepared a special engagement dinner at her restaurant for the Teitelbaums. The table was laden with baked fish, roast duck with home-made stuffing, apple streudel and drinks. Four silver candlesticks graced the table set for the delighted Rivka and Jacob.

Young Shlomo sat beside Jacob, and the two had a lively discussion. Jacob and Rivka were even more impressed with the young man after they had talked and drunk a "l'chaim" for good luck. Shlomo seemed well prepared to begin his own family. Jacob, Rivka, Rachel and Jerome all cheered for their children's good fortune, and a wedding date was set for the young couple.

When the Teitelbaums returned home, they greeted Baila with the news of her betrothal and with congratulations. Baila was stunned, but came to accept her parents' will.

In 1912, Shlomo and Baila were married. The young couple moved in with Baila's parents in Radoszyce where Shlomo apprenticed with his father-in-law who was a shoichet (ritual slaughterer)

Becoming a shoichet is no easy matter. The long learning process involves the careful study of the laws of preparing food that is kosher. The meat eaten by observant Jews must come only from a ritually fit healthy kosher animal that has been painlessly slaughtered by a learned shoichet. After expertly slaughtering the cattle or fowl the shoichet must examine the animal for any disqualifying disease. The profession required the expertise of a veterinarian; and all the complex laws of the Talmud and oral tradition were committed to memory.

On top of the apprenticeship to his father-in-law, Shlomo managed to find the time to study for and pass the rigorous test to become a rabbi.

In 1914, Shlomo was appointed to a position in the small city of Wonchok. Baila was pregnant at the time, and their life seemed very complicated. Not only were they far from home, but World War I had just broken out, and people were stricken with terrible hardships. Parents everywhere were losing their sons as eligible young men were immediately conscripted into the army. Shlomo did not participate in the draft on religious grounds, but he had a rough time hiding out. He was often called a coward and threatened with hanging. But miracles were not as few and far between back then, and somehow Shlomo, Baila and their growing family lived through these harrowing years.

After ten years of marriage, they had two daughters and three sons. Shlomo's mother Rachel had been stricken with typhus during the war and had died relatively young. Shlomo longed for another daughter whom he could name after the mother he had so dearly loved.

That moment arrived for Shlomo in 1924 when I was born. My father went happily to the shul to memorialize his mother by naming me Rachel.

My parents were loving and considerate people. Father almost never raised his voice to mother and was never hurtful or insulting. He always looked at her with a sweet, gentle smile. He was also a wonderful father, so careful to raise us with understanding of and respect for God's ways. He was good to all of us, but I enjoyed his special favor as the youngest girl who bore his beloved mother's name. To this day, I treasure this tangible link to the past.

Several years passed before my family's next big event, my sister Esther's wedding. When she left Wonchok to start a new home with her husband, I began to feel lonely. Esther had always chaperoned me, whether swimming in the summer or sledding in the winter. With her gone, I was surrounded by my brothers. When Mother's work became too much for her, I began to help around the house. I enjoyed the work and learned a great deal about running a household. Mother was always busy at home. She was always mending one of her son's suits, cleaning the shabbos clothes with benzine or creating beautiful hand-stitched pillows. Father took advantage of any spare time to study at the shul.

We all looked forward to Fridays. This day was special in every Jewish home in our town. Each Friday before sunset all the stores closed early. While the streets were deserted, families would be busy washing and changing for Shabbos. My mother would put on a hostess dress, wrap a beautiful kerchief around her head and light the shabbos candles. This gentle glow enhanced the feeling of togetherness, goodness and holiness that we all felt. The singing of the zmiros, Sabbath songs, could be heard in every household.

After the candle lighting, my father and my five brothers would walk to shul. My mother's face shone with pride when she saw her fine sons in their Sabbath finery.

Preparation for Shabbos actually began early on Thursday mornings. All roads leading into the city became crowded with wagons as Polish farmers and peddlers from surrounding villages arrived for yarmark, a farmer's market held in the center of town. The streets buzzed with buying and selling. Mother and I walked from stall to stall admiring the display of fruits, vegetables, chickens, geese, butter, cheese and eggs. I watched as mother carefully picked one of the cackling chickens and then a carp or other white fish as the staples for our meal. As fitting the tradition, my mother saved all week so that she could buy in accordance with the law which states to honor the shabbos with the best food.

I was fascinated to watch Mother place the live carp in a tank of water. I would spend hours watching it circle around in its tank as I fed it a few crumbs. But Friday was the fish's last day, as well as the chicken's. My father took great pride in doing his own slaughtering. With his years of experience, he could immediately tell good from bad, and he would always compliment my mother when she had picked a particularly fine bird.

I watched as Father held the chicken in his hands. Its legs were tied to prevent it from running off. It took hours before one run-away chicken was found in a neighbor's yard.

After the slaughtering Mother went to work plucking the feathers and then soaking and salting the bird. It took almost the entire day, but she rarely complained and was happy that there was enough food to feed her family. By the time I came home from school most of the dishes were ready and the kitchen smells were working on my appetite. My mouth watered from the aroma of chicken, fish, chopped eggs and onions, freshly baked challahs and apple streudel. After eating simple food all week I was eager to sit down to my mother's shabbos feast. But there was still work to be done.

In the summer, when it was too hot to keep the ovens lit, Mother would prepare a cholent, a stew of beef and potatoes. She would then take her cholent to the local baker who would place it in his oven along with the rest of the cholents from all over town. It was my job to place our summer cholent before sunset on Friday. Each woman marked her pot in her own distinct way, but I was always nervous that I would bring home the wrong cholent. Though it was one of my favorite dishes, I didn't cherish the task of going to the steamy bakery to sort through the bubbling pots and retrieve our dinner. The uncomfortably hot chore made me look forward to winter, when we did not have to wait so long for sunset and dinnertime.

During the cold months we had goose, rice, lima beans, applesauce and an egg kichel for dessert, always followed by a glass of hot tea with a cube of sugar.

Even with that treasured little piece of sugar, winter had its drawbacks. Once the sun went down on Friday, we could no longer light a fire in the fireplace. Early on Saturday, a Pole who served as the shabbos goy would go from home to home rekindling the fires that had gone out during the night. It would get so cold by morning that we would stay huddled in our beds until he appeared. I remember how excited I would be to hear his knock at the door. Starting the fire, however, was not so simple. The wood was stored outside and would sometimes be too wet to light. The man would then work with paper and kerosene and would blow and blow until the sparks flew. He was such a thin man that I always wondered how he had the strength to blow so hard. If the fire didn't catch, we would have to eat a cold meal, sing the shabbos songs and crawl back under our bed covers for the day. Most of the time he was good enough to stay and make certain the flames didn't go out.

He was kind of a hero for me, our shabbos goy, and he was given a piece of Sabbath challah for his efforts. He was also paid about twenty cents, but not until Monday, as no money could change hands on the Sabbath. Who ever dreamed that unfriendly non-Jews bearing firebrands would soon come to use us as the fuel in a furnace the size of Europe?

Summer or winter we would wait for my father and brothers to return from shul before the shabbos feast could begin. After the meal, over dessert and tea, we would sit around the table sharing our thoughts and listening to my father's wonderful stories. With his wise and wonderful sense of humor he would entertain us with tales from the Bible, anecdotes from the shul and stories from his childhood.

III

The World in Flames

Such pleasant times were to come to an end, however. In 1939, Hitler declared war, and soon, our city, along with the hundreds of others in Eastern Europe, was in shambles. The shopkeepers had no food to sell and the people went hungry. All the misery that my parents experienced in the First World War was being repeated, but now before my eyes. I wished that it was only another one of their stories. I could not believe that the civilized world I had known and trusted could, in so short a time, become filled with such violent madness.

It was a beautiful fall day in September when the Germans arrived — Friday, at about eleven o'clock in the morning. The sirens had stopped, and everything was deadly quiet. I curiously watched the soldiers march through our gate, led by two patrolmen. I have never forgotten them. They wore large, steel helmets and their uniforms were covered with dust. Their faces were stern, intimidating.

I ran to warn my family, but there was little to be done. Word spread that we would be safer in the villages. Wonchok was near a munitions factory and would therefore be a target. In minutes all the houses were in flames. We ran out through the front gates and joined our neighbors who were also trying to escape the fires. We left everything behind. The only things my mother took were the shabbos candlesticks and the challahs she had baked that morning. Wherever we ended up we could then light the candles and make the blessing over the bread. We had hidden most of our possessions in the basement, expecting to return after the crisis.

I will always remember that Shabbos. All of us from the community were gathered together in a farmer's field. My mother dug a little hole in the earth for the candlesticks, then lit the candles. We all prayed that our homes and belongings would survive the inferno.

All night we watched the smoke-filled sky. The next day we apprehensively trudged back to town. All that remained of our homes were smoking piles of rubble. One of my brothers started to shovel through the ashes in the hopes of recovering some clothing. My mother found some of her silver pieces of dinnerware and was frantically trying to rub them clean. They were hopelessly bent out of shape and blackened beyond repair. I finally convinced her to leave them on the garbage heap of our home. I assured her that they were only material things, and that we still had each other.

I was trying to comfort her, though I, too, felt sick among the charred ruins. I thought this was the worst the war could bring, and that we were all fortunate to have escaped the fate of our material possessions. Little did I know that we were only at the waiting room of Hitler's hell.

With no place to go, we all congregated at our synagogue. Our beautiful little shul stood apart from all the other buildings on the far side of the river, and it had escaped the flames. The synagogue had always made us feel as if something were watching over us, protecting us from evil. Its protection was especially felt at this time as the days of fear and the Days of Awe, the High Holidays, were upon us. Outside the synagogue the river was lined with magnificent trees and wild flowers. How often we would sit on the river's banks dreamily contemplating our distant future instead of the immediate present.

The High Holidays were always very moving, bringing our people together to pray for God's forgiveness and to be inscribed in the Book of Life for the coming year. But that Yom Kippur eve, after the fire, was especially emotional. From the traditional women's balcony, we looked down and watched our men chanting and swaying as they prayed. My father, dressed in white robes, beneath his prayer shawl, led the congregation in the solemn chant. He seemed like an angel to me. I couldn't help but feel proud. My mother glowed too to hear the assemblage compliment her husband's inspiring and melodious prayer. Even though the times were hard, our pride and our dignity were still intact.

The war had turned our beautiful little synagogue into a community shelter. For us there was no other place to go. Everybody was reunited under its roof. We were so packed together that we could hardly move. We heard the children crying for food; we felt their mothers' fear and concern. Some of the boys, including my brothers, dug up potatoes and cooked them in river water. The local farmers would beat up any boys they managed to catch on their grounds.

The fighting lasted only a few days before Poland surrendered. After spending four days crammed together in the synagogue, we were told that the roads were reopened. Stashica

Street, Wonchok's main thoroughfare, led to many other towns, and so throngs of refugees began to pass through our city.

My parents desperately wanted to send me away to a safer placc. But they knew they had to be cautious. Finally, a plan presented itself in the form of a travelling peddlar named Jacob.

Jacob was a plain Jewish man with a good heart, a rickety wagon and a veteran horse. He was passing by when he saw the still-smoking ruins of Wonchok. My parents were thrilled to hear that Jacob had news from the city of Suchedniow, the town in which my big sister lived. Apparently all the people were safe there, and Jacob was headed there the next day. My parents saw this as a stroke of good luck and they asked Jacob to take me along.

Under normal circumstances I would have been happy to go on an excursion to Suchedniow, but after all the family had just been through, I couldn't dream of leaving them. Everything they had worked for lay in ashes. I pitied my parents, but I envied their courage. I will never forget the intense sadness in my father's eye and the distress in my mother's voice when she told Jacob, "Please take care of my baby, Rachela, and take her to my daughter Esther's house."

It was a brisk and bright September morning when we left. I was cold in my thin cotton dress, all I had left at this point. I looked at the sky and prayed that the sun would come out quickly to warm me. I glanced around to say good-bye to the city where I was born and where I'd spent my sheltered youth, surrounded by loving family and friends. A jolt of the wagon jogged me from my reverie.

It took only a day to get to Suchedniow, but it seemed an eternity, I hadn't eaten for days and was feeling dizzy and nauseous. We passed many forests and farms, but no one knew who could help us. Occasionally, I saw German trucks full of singing soldiers. They were celebrating their successful invasion of Poland. I remember thinking that they couldn't be that bad. They were happy and looked so handsome in their uniforms; they were human beings like the rest of us.

I shared the wagon with many boxes and rugs. It was difficult to make a comfortable spot for myself to lie down. Although I wanted desperately to fall asleep and forget my hunger, sleep continued to elude me. Memories of Wonchock and visions of the synagogue kept coming to me. I calmed myself with the knowledge that things would have to get better.

At last, after hours of driving, I was awakened by Jacob's husky voice. He asked me if I knew where we were. It was late in the evening when we finally entered Suchedniow. As we passed through its streets, it seemed that at least one city had escaped the ravages of war. I was grateful for that.

Jacob helped me down from the wagon, disentangling me first from all of his wares. I collapsed when my feet hit the ground. I pulled myself together, shook his hand and thanked him for his kindness in bringing me safely to my sister. With all my strength and courage I went to my sister's dark door, hoping I would find safety in her home.

I quietly knocked on Esther's door and was quickly greeted with cries of concern. The only words I could make out were, "Oh, my God!"

Seeing that I was alone, Esther and her husband Joseph thought the worst. I quickly assured them that my family members were all alive. My sister embraced me, backed away a few steps to look at me, then hurried away to fix me a meal. All the time I ate, she could not take her eyes off me. I could tell that she was working hard to hold back her tears.

With some food in my belly, my hushed sense of relief grew to happiness. My sister only wanted to hear news from home, but I was excitedly exploring the house and playing with my nephews. The boys were so adorable, especially the six-month-old. I was so glad to see that my sister and her husband looked well and that life looked normal once again in my temporary new home.

Finally, the time came for us to sit down and discuss the dramatic events of the war that had begun only five days earlier. Esther and Joseph sought to comfort me by saying that homes and even towns can be rebuilt. As long as the family was intact, we would prevail and soon see happier days.

Seeing that I was exhausted from my long journey, my sister prepared hot water so I could wash and get ready for bed. The beautiful feeling of getting into a bed with soft pillows and down comforters was overwhelming. It was so wonderful not to have to sleep on a hard wooden floor. There were so many aches in my body that I could hardly turn over. Falling asleep, however, did not take long, and I slept for many hours.

My dreams were horrible, filled with images of fire, the sounds of brick and glass being smashed and the scowling faces of our German conquerors. My sister, seeing my torment, helped me pull myself together. She washed the dress I had been wearing for days, and when I put it on and combed my braids I felt like a new person.

Esther took good care of me. She and Joseph had owned a textile shop before the war. They had stock that could be traded on the black market and they were better off than others in the war-ravaged economy. She took me to a dressmaker and had some new clothes made for me. Also having no coat to my name, she bought me a new one. I accompanied her to the market and on the walks she took with my nephews. I began to feel good again, no longer walking with my head down. I could tell that it pleased her to see me getting back to normal.

But everything was different from the last time I had visited only a year ago. The mean faces of the German soldiers were everywhere, and I could not rid myself of the deep feelings of hatred whenever I saw them. Not a day went by without some incident involving the Germans. They frequently dragged people off to work for them.

I did not receive any mail from my parents. But I was delighted to get word that my mother and my youngest brother had gone to stay with my grandparents, while my father and the remainder of the family went to my Aunt Hinda's in Skarzysko.

Life went on. Luckily I had nephews to help me pass the time. I loved them so dearly I could play with them for hours and think of nothing else.

I also had another diversion. His name was Joshua. I first met Joshua in 1938 when I had come to Suchedniow to spend the summer with my sister. Esther and Joseph were practically newlyweds at the time, having only a little five-month-old baby boy. Most of the time that summer was spent with this precious child. I just love babies. In fact, in those days even a bird's or an insect's life was precious to me. I spent endless hours contemplating the miracle of life that God had created. I loved to watch my little nephew smiling and to hear him babbling his first words. Trying to understand his attempts at speech and guiding him through his first tentative steps brought me pleasure. However, another pleasure was beginning to make itself known to me.

Joshua lived with his parents and his sister, Sara, downstairs from Esther and Joseph. Sara and I became good friends during the vacation. When I went a flight down to visit her, I also had the opportunity to catch a glimpse of her cute brother.

Joshua hardly even noticed me that summer. Nevertheless, I felt my heart fill with excitement every time I looked at him. It was a new feeling, like a flame growing within. Joshua was tall with broad shoulders and curly black hair that peeked out from beneath a cap worn titled back. His whole face lit up when he smiled. But, unfortunately, I was too young for him — only fourteen — and so my first love had to stay a secret.

That vacation ended and I returned home. Now the war had come, and those carefree teenage years had come to an abrupt close. Yet here I was, once again, living upstairs from Joshua.

The cold weather was rapidly approaching, and the days grew shorter. During the long winter nights there was nothing to do. All social activities were prohibited, and it was forbidden to be out past curfew. When my brother-in-law invited friends from the building to join him in a chess game, the house livened up a bit. Before settling down for a game, everyone exchanged views of the war.

The object of my affections, Joshua, was especially outspoken on the subject. He always predicted a quick end to the war, and his optimism made me feel good. During those chess games, I looked for any excuse to walk over and be close to him. To me, he was the brightest and best-looking boy in the world.

One evening Joshua actually spoke to me. He called me over and asked me what my plans were if the war were to end soon. I told him that I would go back to school. He was just mildly interested in my academic aspirations, but I was perfectly thrilled that he was, at least, paying some attention to me.

Every time I heard Joshua's knock I dropped what I was doing and ran to open the door for him. I found great pleasure in simply stealing a glance at him.

Despite my sister's hospitality and my excitement of having a first boyfriend, I still longed to be back with my parents. They were also concerned about bringing me back home. Esther and Joseph had only a two-room apartment and I was impinging on their privacy.

Finally, in March of 1940, my parents wrote to me urging me to join them. After six months of living with my sister, it was difficult to say goodbye. I remember the sadness in Esther's eyes when it came time for me to leave. She couldn't even speak as she swallowed back tears. She held her baby while Joseph held the older boy. I kissed them all before I boarded the train. As it pulled out of the Suchedniow station, they waved to me, throwing kisses. How quickly the time had gone. I sat on the train thinking about the winter months just passed, wondering, too, if Joshua would be there the next time I visited. Little did I know that he and I would meet again — not in the pleasant company of my sister and her family, but in a concentration camp. Such thoughts were still unimaginable in 1940.

IV

Between the Ghetto Walls

My parents had chosen to settle in Skarzysko, their native city. It was no happy reunion, as few pleasant memories remained for them there. My mother's family had long ago moved to Radoszyce. My father's father had passed away at an early age, and the rest of the family was now scattered throughout Poland. Only one of my father's sisters, Aunt Hinda, remained. As she had lived in Skarzysko all her life, she had many connections and was able to help us get an apartment.

The train trip did not take long, and I was soon stepping off at Skarzysko Station to see my brother, Zisman. I was thrilled to see him, and we could hardly wait to exchange news.

I had last visited my father's family when I was ten years old, and those pleasant memories contrasted with what I saw around me. The city was extremely grim. Most of the streets were closed, and the March cold kept the high-piled snow from melting.

I couldn't wait to get to my parents' apartment, but Zisman told me not to expect too much. He said that we had been lucky to get any apartment at all. He also said that he had learned to accept the situation, and that I would too. After all, there was a war going on.

Zisman then pointed to a building a short distance ahead, and my heart began to pound as I recognized the outline of my parents in one of the windows. Our reunion was filled with joy, but my brother had been right. There certainly was a war going on. The signs were everywhere. The apartment was bleak and barren; there was no furniture, but for some beds, a table and some chairs lent to us by Aunt Hinda.

My parents saw the disappointment on my face and comforted me by saying that everything would soon be back to normal. The war would end shortly, and we would rebuild our home and buy everything new.

We later sat down to talk about the time I'd spent in Suchedniow. My parents were eager to hear about their grandchildren. I could see how much they missed Esther and her family. I began to miss my wider social life in Suchedniow.

My older brother Beryl was not with the family in Skarzysko. Because he did not show promise in school, Beryl had been sent

off to apprentice with a watchmaker in Starachowice. This was a more promising profession than the usual shoemaker, tailor or carpenter trade then open to Polish Jews. Beryl took great pride in his work, and was soon able to take apart and put together complex timepieces. His skills allowed him the opportunity to make frequent visits before the war, but now even mail was a questionable proposition.

Beryl was prepared to join the family here, but our tiny apartment in Skarzysko could hardly accommodate him. Not to burden us, he relocated to the larger city of Ostrowiec where he had better business opportunities. As a Jew, however, he would have immediately been taken away by the Nazis for forced labor. Fortunately, his thick auburn hair, light brown eyes and freckled, snub nose gave him the option of posing as a Catholic Pole. He bought an identity card from the black market and took on the name of Josef Kowalski. He began to get steady clients from the German soldiers stationed at Ostrowiec, but getting to us in Skarzysko became more and more difficult. We soon lost touch with Beryl altogether.

With less siblings around and no friends, each day in Skarzysko was another exercise in loneliness and boredom. I was sixteen. I wanted to explore life, not to be denied new vistas and experiences.

It was weeks before I became accustomed to the strange, new city. I resented being away from my childhood friends. I missed my little hometown of Wonchok where every corner was familiar.

Skarzysko was bigger than my hometown. It had a large Jewish population and a modern school system with higher education. Many Jewish boys in Skarzysko enjoyed studying sacred texts in well-reputed Yeshivas. The city was known for its industry and its major railroad connections.

Skarzysko was one of the luckier cities, as it had not been devastated by the war. Families still had their homes intact, and that was the most important thing. The year 1940, however, ushered in a new law that greatly changed the face of the city. A ghetto was established to segregate Jews from Christians.

The skarzysko ghetto had its own committee or gemienda. This elite group of Jews, hand-picked by the Germans, was responsible for governing our people. Permits were needed for all kinds of things. For example, the Jewish cemetery was located on the Christian side of town. So permits were required to hold Jewish funerals there. No Jews could leave the ghetto without the proper permit from the committee members. These Jews enjoyed only a little power, as they had to report directly to the German police. For the most part they spoke up for us to the ruling tyrants.

Only a person who has lived through our circumstances can fully understand what the word "ghetto" means. Hunger and fear hung over every square of the ghetto. Fear of attack, fear of disease — every aspect of life was marked by fear. We never knew what the next day would bring, for each morning new laws affecting our lives were enacted:

Jews must wear the yellow star.

Jews are forbidden to ride the railway.

Jews must be indoors by seven in the evening.

With all that we still felt that as long as we had each other we should be thankful. More and more suspicious incidents were reported, however. People were whisked away for no reason. "Executions" or murders took place regularly. With time, we all became accustomed to the hell of ghetto life. We had no choice. I began to visit Aunt Hinda more frequently to help my two little cousins with their education. There were no schools for Jews in the ghetto, so all learning had to take place at home. My aunt also started to visit us more often, which helped make the days a bit more bearable.

My father had some friends who also came to visit us during the day. One was particularly close. His name was Joseph. The two men constantly discussed the war. I remember how upset my father was over the collapse of France in 1940. We lived with the hope of a quick end to the war, and events such as France's surrender to Germany did not bode well.

Then, in 1941, the Russian Air Force suffered a crushing defeat at the hands of the German Luftwaffe. Even though the Germans had penetrated the Soviet Union, my father was still confident that the Allies would beat them back. He kept insisting that America, the greatest country in the world, would enter the war any day and stop Hitler in his course of destruction.

I dreamed that some day I would wake up and find a world at peace. I was too young to live within walls that tightened on us every day.

In 1941, my mother became ill. I had never seen her bedridden. She had always been so full of vitality, spending her hours cooking, cleaning and supervising the household. Suddenly, she was an invalid. She breathed with great difficulty and her condition deteriorated daily.

My worried father sent me to get our ghetto physician, Dr. Feldman. His examination revealed that Mother had developed a serious heart condition. I was completely devastated. I followed the doctor to the door and asked as many questions as I could. The doctor merely looked at me as if the angel of death had appeared before his eyes.

"My dear, your mother is not going to live. Her kidneys are malfunctioning. She is retaining a great deal of water which will eventually reach her heart. She is going to die."

Listening to the doctor, I felt as though it was me he was sentencing to death. When I regained my composure, I saw that the doctor was trying to console me. He knew that I was religious.

"Listen," he said. "Don't you believe in God?"

I nodded my head and answered, "I wish you did. If you believed in God you would tell me to have faith that my mother will live." I began to sob as I walked away.

Back home everyone gathered around me anxious for the doctor's report on Mother's condition. My lips moved, but nothing came out. My face quickly whitened and I felt dizzy. Everyone guessed Mother's fate, but I just couldn't say the words. I already felt orphaned, empty and unwanted in this wide, cold world.

I decided to visit my aunt and uncle, and to tell them of Mother's condition. They comforted me and reassured me by telling me that Dr. Feldman was known for his indifference toward patients. They urged me to seek a second opinion, recommending a Dr. Breshinski. He had an excellent reputation, but was now too old to get around with ease. On top of this, he was not Jewish and could very well refuse to come to the ghetto to see my mother. Despite the difficulties I began the long procedure of obtaining permission for a visit to this doctor on the Christian side of the city.

We would certainly need funds for the enterprise, and with the seriousness of Mother's condition we sought new ways to seek brother Beryl living undercover in Ostrowiec. My plucky little brother Shmulek volunteered for the dangerous mission of locating Josef Kowalski, Beryl's Catholic identity. With his non-Jewish looks and young age, Shmulek was the best choice to risk removing the mandatory Star of David armband and to travel outside the ghetto. We were less concerned about the Germans than we were about the Poles who might recognize little Shmulek as a Jew. There were posters everywhere offering rewards of one kilo of sugar to any Poles who turned Jews in to the German authorities. Sadly, many tons of sugar were claimed.

A determined young lad, Shmulek finally succeeded in tracking down his older brother. Beryl was able to give Shmulek a sum of money to take home, and promised to visit the family and his ailing mother as soon as he was able. We were all relieved when Shmulek returned home safely with his mission accomplished. We were grateful for Beryl's financial help, and hoped that he'd be able to risk a visit to us before Mother's health deteriorated any further.

My mother was not the only sick one in the family. My aunt Hinda's young daughter, also named Rachel, was bedridden and fighting a dangerously high fever. My aunt was filled with hope that her child would recover soon. As I left Aunt Hinda's apartment Dr. Feldman's ominous words, "Your mother is going to die," reverberated through my head. I felt that the Nazis would kill us all with the diseases fostered by their wretched occupation. Only when I remembered my aunt's courageous optimism did the heaviness lift from my heart.

At home, the family sat around Mother's bed listening to her heavy breathing. Father's eyes were red and weary from lack of sleep. He was spending more and more time studying Talmud in an attempt to distract himself from the worsening situation. I wanted to speak to my family about how I felt, but emotion clogged my throat.

I waited impatiently for the next morning when I could pay a visit to Dr. Breshinski. My uncle and I had received special permission to leave the ghetto, and Beryl's money would be needed to pay and bribe our way to the doctor's door and good graces.

The next day, we were greeted at the door by the physician's wife. Though I poured out my heart to her, she was reluctant to allow Jews in to see her husband. The doctor overheard our conversation, however, and asked me to step into his office.

Dr. Breshinski had the look of a wealthy aristocrat, dressed in his long white medical coat and holding a black and silver cigarette holder. It was evident that he was a sensitive and compassionate man. He told me to be seated and asked me to repeat everything that Dr. Feldman had said about my mother's condition. He reminded me that he was not God and could not work miracles, but that as a skilled doctor he would try to save my mother. He agreed to come to the ghetto with my uncle and me and was actually quite flattered that we had gone to such trouble to seek him out. He treated my mother over several weeks and, miraculously, her health began to rapidly improve. Despite his words to the contrary, Dr. Breshinski was, at least, a godsend.

It was wonderful to see Mother's vitality return. I filled her in on all the news she had missed. She looked into my eyes, smiled softly and thanked me for being a good daughter. I began to wonder about my mother's state of mind. She spoke of disturbing dreams concerning the rest of our family. She was worried about her parents, as well. When I told her about little Rachela's illness, she insisted that I go to her immediately because she also had a terrible premonition about the child's fate.

My aunt's house felt dark and empty like a mausoleum. It made me uneasy. My aunt came to the door and greeted me with red, swollen eyes.

Little Rachela lay in bed motionless, her mouth wide open. My aunt had tried to breathe air into her baby's lungs, but it was hopeless. She sadly explained how she had tried various methods to reduce the girl's fever. But the child was now near death. I stared solemnly at my beloved cousin and wondered how such a beautiful child could be taken from this world. Though I knew the answer lay only with God, I could not help bitterly thinking that sometimes He acts unjustly.

My aunt asked me to watch my cousin while she went to get more alcohol. I touched Rachela's small hand and spoke to her, praying that my aunt would not leave us alone for too long. All of a sudden, Rachela fluttered her blue eyes several times. It seemed as if she were trying to communicate, but she couldn't speak. Then her eyes opened once again and stared past me. She was dead, but I had no idea. I had never seen a dead person before. I kept talking to the child, holding her still warm hand.

When Aunt Hinda finally returned and saw that her baby wasn't moving, she began to slap Rachela's face. She began to scream, "I've lost my life, my little girl, my little girl is lost." Hinda's husband stood by like a stone figure.

Their little Rachela was gone, and one more painful image was etched into my memory.

In a cloud of despair, I found my way home. My mother had only to look at my face to know that her horrible dream had come true. She held me in her arms as I wept.

"But she didn't look dead," I cried. "Her eyes were wide open. She was looking at the wall behind me. Why do people die like that? With their eyes open?"

"Perhaps they want to take a last look at the world," Mother answered.

Wounds heal and sorrows pass. My aunt and uncle never fully recovered from the loss of their daughter, but they began to visit us more frequently and take comfort in our company.

Mother's heart condition continued to improve. Dr. Breshinski had prescribed lots of rest, and Mother continued to spend a great deal of time in bed. Friends and relatives spoke of nothing but politics and of the growing number of people being dragged off by the Germans.

My parents were afraid for two of my brothers, Beryl and Leible, who were living on their own in different cities. My father feared for his brother who lived with his wife and three children in Warsaw. My uncle was serving in the Polish army, and we hadn't heard from him in quite a while. My mother, in turn, worried about her parents. I tried to convince my mother that she hadn't heard from her family because it was forbidden for Jews to write to each other. I wanted to comfort her and allay her fears, as I knew she couldn't stand much more heartache. Though life consisted mainly of worries about food, health, and German decrees, things seemed to stabilize and the days passed quickly.

For a while our evenings remained socially active. Friends would gather at my brother's to play chess. This gave them the chance to exchange thoughts and to keep their minds occupied. But then an earlier curfew was imposed and even that pleasure was denied them. From seven at night until five in the morning, anyone caught on the street without a permit could be shot on the spot. No questions were asked. After seven, the streets became as quiet as a graveyard. Our nights became miserable.

One afternoon, a young man named Yitzchak came over and introduced himself. He suggested that it would be better if we spoke outside. At first I could not understand why he wanted to talk to me privately, but then he explained. He had regards from my brother Beryl and my grandfather Jacob. I couldn't believe my ears and wanted desperately to run to my parents with the news.

"Listen, Miss Walshaw," he said, "Your brother asked me not to mention anything to his parents, because he was afraid they would only worry." He then told of the horrible circumstances that had brought my brother and grandfather together.

Now my Grandfather Jacob was a ritual slaughterer in his hometown of Radoshice. During the war, this was a forbidden practice and an dangerous profession, but there was a great demand for Kosher meat by the Jews who were eager to obtain some meat or poultry to celebrate a holiday or other special occasion. So my grandfather risked his life to slaughter for some Jewish neighbors in his own home.

Eventually, Grandpa was caught and arrested by the SS. We discovered that he was dragged out of a Passover Seder, charged with slaughtering contraband chickens for the holiday. The family did not know where he had been taken or what had happened to him since his disappearance. Not until that morning in 1941.

Yitzchak, the source of this invaluable information, was a native of our city who knew our parents as well as my brother. While working at the railway station one day, he watched a train roll by that was densely packed with Jews. Yitzchak approached desperately seeking a familiar face. Disregarding the risk, he ran up to a car whose windows were open. There was my brother Beryl, waving frantically to him, eager to tell someone about the atrocities he had witnessed in Skarzysko. When Beryl contacted Yitzchak, he told him in a few rushed words that he knew his mother was sick and that he wished he could come home. He was identified as a Jew outside the ghetto and was being shipped away, at best, for forced labor.

On the very same car as my brother, Yitzchak saw an elderly man standing at the window, also trying to tell him something.

He said that his daughter lived in the city and to please send word to her. Yitzchak got the address and asked him who his family was.

"My daughter is Baila, married to Shlomo Walshaw." At this point, Beryl turned around, stunned. "Listen," he said to the elderly man, "Baila and Shlomo Walshaw are my parents!" Yitzchak watched in shock and confusion as Grandfather, with deep emotion, turned around and took his grandson Beryl in his arms. Crying, he said, "My child, what are you doing here among the doomed?"

That was the last that Yitzchak saw and heard as the train picked up speed and moved away. It was a tragic coincidence that my grandfather met his grandson in such circumstances. He hadn't seen him since my sister's wedding, and now there he was, a handsome young man of eighteen, looking so different than he had years ago. It was a brief, bittersweet moment that they shared before arriving at their final destination, which Yitzchak knew to be Auschwitz.

Yitzchak stopped talking when he saw that I was trembling, but I begged him to continue. Unfortunately, he knew nothing more. Beryl's train pulled away, its destination — Auschwitz — unknown to the passengers.

"How pitiful," I said to Yitzchak. "If my mother knew that Beryl was sent away while trying to see her, she would die on the spot." I thanked him for his consideration, and he told me how sorry he was to be the bearer of such sad news. His brother-in-law had also been sent away, so he knew how I must feel.

"We're all in the same boat," he said. "Goodbye. Perhaps the next time we meet, you will have heard better news from them."

What good news could I expect to hear? News from Auschwitz, the place where innocent people were sent and tortured for no reason? None of us knew yet of actual death camps. We only knew that people were disappearing, never to return.

Then nights were long, and I would fall asleep thinking about my brother and grandfather. I remembered Grandpa as a handsome man with a brilliant smile and strong, sensitive features. I wondered why he had been taken away, and I felt pity for my grandmother. She, too, was alone, fretting the night away. Many questions came to mind. Was there really a God who watched over us? How could something like this happen to a man like my grandfather, seventy-two years old? He spent most of his time in shul studying the Talmud and biblical commentary. Surely he didn't deserve to suffer so. He should have been allowed to live out his life and face death with dignity. And my brother Beryl, eighteen years old. He had only wanted to see his mother. He risked his life to ride on a train. How could such a minor thing erase a person from the face of this earth?

My mother was quite a mind reader. "What is the matter, my child?" she asked. "You don't seem right. Aren't you feeling well?"

"Yes, Mother," I said. "How do you feel?"

"I could be better, but thank God for that."

"What about the dreams?" I asked. "Do you still have them?"

"Yes, my child," she answered sadly. "The same horrible dream every night. There's just one thing I can't understand. Why does my son Beryl call for help in my dreams?"

I swallowed hard but did not share the horrible news with her.

I looked out of the window and admired the beautiful, bright sun, the blooming trees and the blue sky. Spring had arrived, and the world looked fresh and newborn. I was inspired to think about the future.

Would there ever be enough food to satisfy our hunger? Would the gates even be open for us to walk freely? I could find no answers to these questions and I started to become bitter. Religious people, I felt, were living in a fantasy world. They waited patiently for the Messiah to come while the madness continued all around them.

My father continued to pray. It seemed that he was on speaking terms with God, so I asked him why God didn't punish the monster who had destroyed so many lives for no reason. My father replied, "We shall live to witness the end. Hitler will wind up like Haman, you wait and see." Then he cautioned me about turning against God and becoming bitter.

I knew how much my father loved me and how much he grieved when I was unhappy. I tried to convince myself that there must be some reason that so many loved ones had been torn from us, even if I could not see it. Though I wanted to believe that this new season would usher in the bright and beautiful future of my dreams, I would have to dream on.

The weeks and months passed rapidly. More bad news hit our ghettos. New laws were imposed and the first labor camps were built. Young men were forced to leave their families to go to work in these labor camps. There was an increase of sadistic violence against Jews. We were being crushed to death between the ghetto walls.

V

Cousin Zisman, Brother Zisman

Late one afternoon a small boy approached our house. For a moment I thought he was a beggar, but he told me that he was my cousin, Zisman, from Warsaw. I took him to my parents who embraced him. Then they backed away to take a good look at their nephew.

Zisman was in a terrible state. His clothes were torn from his bony body; his face was filthy and his feet were covered with blisters from walking. My mother fixed him a light meal, washed him and sent him off to bed.

We hovered over the boy as he rested, anxious to know what had happened to his family. He told his story slowly.

His father, my father's brother, died fighting for the Polish army. Then their house was bombed. His mother, along with two small children, remained in the Warsaw Ghetto. Zisman, the oldest, was left to care for the family. They were living with ten other families and were dying of hunger when typhus hit. Zisman wanted to stay and nurse his stricken family back to health, but his mother pleaded with him to leave the ghetto before he, too, fell ill. Zisman wanted to obey, but being only ten years old he was afraid to leave his family. His mother convinced him that he could only take care of them if he stayed alive. "If any of us should die," she told Zisman, "the survivors must find each other. There must be a family again to carry on the name."

And so Zisman planned his escape through the city gates. He wandered through the Polish countryside for two months before he reached us. Those months had been harrowing for him. He slept in farmers' barns and ate the food thrown out for the cows and pigs. The Polish farmers allowed him shelter, and for that he was grateful.

I looked to my father for his reaction. His face was pale as he asked Zisman if his father had been buried at a Jewish cemetery. Unfortunately, Zisman did not know for sure. Father then took up his prayer book to pray for the soul of his perished brother.

I pitied my little cousin. His only hope was that his mother, brothers and sisters were still alive. I began to think that maybe he shouldn't have left them. But we all tried to convince him that he had done the right thing. My father spoke to him in his most tender manner, telling him to have faith. "For the Jewish people, as long as there is life, there is hope," he said.

Plagued with guilt, Zisman cried to my father, "I will never forgive myself for leaving them. As soon as I am strong enough, I will make the journey back home." But Zisman's strength did not return. My mother noticed that he had trouble even getting out of bed in the morning. As a mother will do, she put her hand to his forehead and felt that his head was hot. Her face was strained as she told me, "Rachela, please stay away from Zisman; he probably has typhus."

What did I know of typhus? My mother had seen it kill so many during the First World War, but I was only concerned with helping my cousin. His fever was rising, and I would go to him when he called out during the night for cold compresses.

One night when I went to him, I felt a chill pass through my body. For a moment, remembering my mother's warning, I was afraid. But I let it pass and ignored it. The next day, my family was so busy bustling around the house that it took awhile for them to notice I was still in bed.

It was a hot day in August, 1941. The sun shone brightly through the window, causing my fever to rise even higher. I had terrible chills and an unbearable headache. My brother Shmulek complained about the same symptoms. The icy cold compresses which mother repeatedly applied to our heads only helped a little. We had come down with typhus. Again Zisman had to suffer guilt, as he had brought the dreaded disease to our home. My mother was terrified; my father anguished. I stifled my cries as best I could, for I loved my parents and couldn't stand to see them so distraught.

I myself was unable to think about how seriously I was affected. My mother held my hands and tried to help me. She asked my permission to cut off my braids, promising that it would help relieve the headaches. I loved my long hair, but it the end I had to give in.

I lay in bed racked with pain. My eyes could hardly focus. I could hear the commotion going on in the house, but it sounded far away. The news spread quickly. Everyone was alarmed that our visitor from Warsaw had infected the ghetto.

Soon, several Jewish policemen entered our house with a warrant from the Jewish Committee. We were to be placed in quarantine. Typhus is a contagious disease, and it could spell disaster for the entire ghetto if any others were infected. I was terribly frightened.

There was a little cheder or schoolroom that, at the start of the war, had been turned into a hospital to serve the ghetto. It then became the isolation ward where Zisman, Shmulek and I were taken by the policeman. To make matters worse, our apartment was sealed off and a notice was posted on the door forbidding anyone to enter.

It was early in the afternoon when we were lifted onto the stretchers. A crowd had gathered to watch, and the people craned their necks trying to get a look at us. My parents had stood by, horrified at the scene. My heart was pounding like a trip-hammer. My father tried to console me. "My dear children," he called after us. "Don't worry. You will be fine. With God's help, I will see you all again soon." Through eyes glazed with fever, I could make out the sad faces of my parents as they watched us being carried away.

The "hospital" was a bare, one-room building whose four beds had straw mattresses. The closest thing to a doctor was an army medic from the First World War. He took our temperature but gave us no medicine. The fever had left us so thirsty. The three of us cried and cried for water. But no one answered. A Jewish watchman was stationed outside the hospital to make certain that no one entered.

During this time, my parents and my two brothers. Zisman and Moishe, stayed with Aunt Hinda. Mother tried to come every day to bring us warm tea and cold compresses, but the watchman gave her a hard time. Visiting was strictly forbidden, but Mother somehow managed to get in to help nurse us back to health.

One day a tall man with a briefcase came to visit. I thought he was a doctor, but he shook my hand and told me he was the barber.

"What do you want?" I asked him.

With a polite smile, he explained that he had been sent to cut off my hair. He apologized saying that he had to follow orders. He told me that I must try to understand the situation and not fight him. But I did fight. I screamed and fought with all my remaining strength, but it was to no avail. In minutes, my head was shaved.

When my mother saw what had happened she was shaken. I could hardly see her through my tears, and I couldn't talk since my throat was so sore from screaming.

On Mother's next visit, she brought me a beautiful kerchief which she wrapped around my head. In her tender mother's voice she offered what consolation she could.

"My dear child, do you know how fast hair grows? In no time your hair will be beautiful again. Even more beautiful than before."

I threw myself into her arms, sobbing. Through my shame, I realized why my mother had been so insistent on cutting my braids. She had only wanted to ease the pain of this moment. To this day I remember her gentle wisdom and the touch of her cool fingers stroking my face.

After five or six days, the fever broke. Day by day, the three of us began to recover, and, after two weeks in confinement, we were finally well enough to leave the ward.

The population of Skarzysko grew so steadily that the food supply became a major problem. We felt less fortunate than even the animals. A cat or dog was, at least, free to roam the city in search of food. The Jews were limited to the ghetto. One did not dare venture beyond its walls without a permit.

Many young people had no choice but to resort to trading on the black market. Smuggling, with all its risk and danger, became a way of life. There were few stores left. There were no butchers, no bakers, no dry goods and rations were not dependable. People who had managed to hide some of their goods were able to trade with the Poles who still had free access to the ghetto.

We were fortunage that my brother Shmulek sorted
potatoes for the German police. The Germans appeared to
be quite satisfied with his work. Taking pity on him, they
gave Shmulek permission to take the bad potatoes home
with him. And so we subsisted, more or less, on this one
versatile food. It was amazing how many dishes Mother
could create with just potatoes. Aware that others were not
so lucky, my parents happily shared our fortune with our
neighbors.

Besides food, the most difficult commodity for us to get
was wood or coal. And without fuel for cooking, the potatoes
were useless. But God was looking after us. My brother
Moishe worked at the railway station loading coal onto
wagons. Each day he would hide a small piece on his pants
or under his jacket and bring it home to us. This little bit
was enough to help us survive.

A fire in the stove also gave us life on cold winter days. It
brought the family together and warmed our hearts as well
as our bodies. My oldest brother, Zisman, taught me songs
and delighted us all with his stories. Mother took great pride
in watching us try to bring cheer into our miserable little
ghetto apartment.

Zisman was a born storyteller. He loved to ramble on
about his childhood, and one incident, in particular, comes
to mind when I think of him. The story was comic, though
it was very nearly a tragedy.

My brother Zisman was about seven at the time and
studying in a cheder. One freezing day when the temperature dipped below zero, Zisman and two other boys his age
decided to have a little fun after school. About a quarter of
a mile from home was a frozen lake where youngsters skated.

The ice looked beautiful, covered with many natural designs and protruding frozen hedges. Zisman practiced his skating on the edge of his shoes.

Suddenly his face was covered with fear. A little piece of ice had broken off and little Zisman fell into the freezing lake. He panicked, scrambling to hold onto the remaining ice while screaming for help. His friends reached in and with all their strength finally pulled him out.

Safe but shivering, Zisman now worried that he would be punished by our parents. So he decided to run as fast as he could with his soaking clothes still frozen to his body. He headed for the synagogue, where a fire burned all day and where he could hide as his clothing dried.

Since young and old alike were called to God's house to do His work and study the Talmud, Zisman rationalized that this justified his seeking refuge at the synagogue. When he arrived, he took off his clothes and put them in front of the fire. It took hours for them to dry. When night fell, my father arrived at the synagogue for his evening prayers. Imagine his surprise when he saw his son, hidden in the shadows, stark naked!

At first, Father was angry. But when he heard that Zisman had nearly drowned in the lake, he softened. He was only upset that he hadn't known where his son had disappeared to and had thought all along that he was playing at his friend's home.

Zisman grew up to be bright and understanding, a fine speaker and a devoted son. Even today, I miss my brother who taught me so many things and gave me so many beautiful memories.

Even my brother's pleasant stories could not dispel the harsh reality of our lives. It took me some time to recover my health. Cousin Zisman lived only for the day that he would be well enough to travel home. I had only to look at my cousin to realize how lucky I was to be home and safe with my family.

To keep Zisman from dwelling on his past, my father took matters into his own hands. He noted that Zisman had neglected his Hebrew lessons since the war had started. It was time for a ten-year-old boy to begin studying for his bar mitzvah. So my father tried to instruct him. But who could understand the boy's pain? Zisman tried but he was too plagued by guilt to pay attention to my father's lessons.

One day, after many weeks of staying with us, he decided he could wait no longer. I still remember the sadness of that day. When it came time to part, I couldn't say goodbye. I bit my finger to keep back a tear and dashed away from his sad eyes. He departed alone into the darkness. We all worried about this young boy in poor health wandering from city to city, forced to hide his Jewish identity at all costs.

Meanwhile I struggled to regain strength. Days and weeks passed and I started to feel better, especially as my hair had grown in a few inches. I was no longer ashamed to walk outside to get a little sunshine and to visit friends.

As winter approached, I would curl up in a corner and listen to my father's enchanting, melodic voice as he studied the Talmud. I would also listen to the marvelous stories my oldest brother Zisman would tell on breaks from his rabbinical lessons. He had such a way with words that he would make even simple events sound exciting. In spite of the horror around us, he dreamed of a happy future. He had faith in God.

He helped me keep the hope alive that the war would end and things would certainly get better. I also prayed to

God that my little cousin would find his way to the Warsaw Ghetto and safely reach his family.

VI

Leible the Scholar

My brother Leible was next to the oldest. I didn't spend much time with him during my childhood. Shortly after his Bar Mitzvah he decided, with my parents' permission, to leave home. He wanted to become a rabbinic scholar.

In 1933 he attended a Yeshiva in the city of Ostrowiec. We were all so delighted to see him when he made his annual visits home. While studying there, he stayed with a family whom our parents funded to provide him with food and personal care.

But Leible was not satisfied with the Yeshiva's academic level. He wanted a school of higher learning, so after a year he applied and was accepted to Warsaw Yeshiva. This school had a more modern dormitory and was better staffed and equipped.

I admired the family scholar so much — with his handsome face, dark blond hair and hazel eyes. My parents were happy to have the whole family together again when Leible returned from Warsaw after two years. We had all missed him very much. Leibel, with his fiercely independent and intellectually curious mind, was so different from my other brothers. He had "conquered" Warsaw Yeshiva and was desperate to get into Lubliner Yeshiva, the top academy for Jewish scholars. My parents were delighted when he was accepted and felt sure that he would become a great scholar.

Two years later, in 1939, the rumor spread that Germany would soon start a war with Poland. My parents feared for their son who was so far away from home. He honored his parents' wishes and returned immediately.

Leible was nineteen at the time, mature and very learned. He was respected by all of his hometown friends and acquaintances who were impressed by his erudite speech and eloquent conversation. It was a pleasure just to sit and listen to him. He had a brilliant rabbinical career ahead of him, but that September the Germans took over Poland and changed everyone's plans. As we gathered in the refuge of our synagogue, many of our townspeople thinking they would be safer farther away from the city, departed for a small Jewish farm settlement a few miles away. Among them was my brother Leibel.

Shmeryl and his wife Cilia owned one of those farms. Leible stayed with them, their daughter and five sons after he learned that the city of Wonchok had been burned down and his home destroyed. The village had many Jewish families but no educational facilities, so Leible was asked to stay on and teach the children.

My parents weren't too happy that my brother was living with Shmeryl and Cilia, but as their home was gone, they could offer him no alternative. Each one of us had to go different ways. I was lucky enough to be able to stay with Esther and Joseph during that time. Father, Zisman, Beryl and Moishe went to Hinda's; Mother and Shmulek went to her parents in Radoszyce.

After the family was eventually resettled in Skarzysko, Leible came home for a visit. Our parents were thrilled that after so many months we were finally reunited. But Mother saw that her twenty-year old son Leible was not happy. He acted strangely confused and preoccupied.

He had spent most of his time in the farm village teaching Shmeryl's sons and daughter along with the other children from the village who would otherwise have to travel to the city for an education. Naturally, they were delighted to have a teacher of Leible's caliber in their midst.

Shmeryl was a farmer, but not a poor man. He had plenty of acreage and a big heart to match. He helped many poor people, including itinerant beggars. Shmeryl's door was always open to them, and he fed them generously.

Mother's concern was not for Leible's stomach, but for his heart. My mother wanted her son to marry a scholar's daughter rather than a farmer's daughter. Sure enough, Leible had fallen in love with Shmeryl's daughter, Rivka. Mother spent hours trying to convince Leible not to get involved, but to have patience and to wait at least until the end of the war. Still, Leible, the giant intellect, followed his heart and begged his mother for permission to marry Rivka.

"Mother," he said, "I understand your concerns for my future career, but I must live in the present. And at present, I am madly in love with Rivka. I cannot live without her! But I also love and respect you, my parents. Dear Mother, try to understand how much I love this woman — she is everything to me. Without her, my life has no meaning!"

Mother embraced him, and her eyes filled with tears as she said, "My precious, gifted son, I want so much for you. I can't see how tying you down to a farm will make you happy!"

Father wasn't as adamant on the question of Leible's marriage. He was consumed with his fight to survive and provide for his family. He was disgusted with the war and angry with himself for falling victim to these circumstances. He consented without much discussion to Leible's marriage. Leible left us to return to the farm where his heart belonged, back to his loving Rivka. They were married in a small ceremony and Leible continued to live with his new in-laws.

In 1940, all the Jewish farmers had to give up their land. They were ordered to take some personal belongings and were sent to a city called Wierzbnik. By the following year, a ghetto was formed and life was reduced to the barest existence.

In 1941, Rivka gave birth to a baby boy. Leibel was optimistic that his newborn son would bring them good luck. Meanwhile, he was toiling daily one mile from Wierzbnik in a small town called Starachowice. It was known for its ammunition factory where all the young men of the area were forced to work. Leible worked hard there, but he didn't mind. As long as he could come home to see Rivka, he was happy.

Then the German commandant gave orders to build a concentration camp. In no time at all, Starachowice Lager was established, and Leible was a prisoner within its fences.

In September of 1942, rumors began spreading among the prisoners that Wierzbnik would soon be evacuated. Signs were posted stating that anyone who tried to escape from the camp would be captured and executed.

Leible, meanwhile, had no news from his wife. He was heart-broken to be separated from his loving Rivka and their precious baby. He was prepared to risk his own life in order to join them.

Leible's attempt to escape from camp was unsuccessful. He was quickly caught and brought back. The German commander interrogated him: "What was your reason for trying to escape?"

Leible replied, "My only reason was to be with my wife and baby during their evacuation."

The Commander ordered Leible to take off his pants and, in front of the assembled prisoners, he proceeded to whip him twenty-five times on his back and sexual organs until blood flowed and he was near death.

His fellow inmates carried him to his bunk. Throughout the night they applied compresses to his wounds to help bring down the swelling. In the morning the kapo ordered him to leave, under a directive from the German commandant. Leible gathered all his remaining strength. At last he would be with his loving wife and baby. All three of them were sent to Treblinka where they perished in the gas chambers along with hundreds of thousands of other Jews.

The final chapter of Leible's tragic story was told to me after the war by my friend Manny, a neighbor from my home town. He was there to witness the torture that my brother endured. Manny was lucky to be a survivor of the camp, and we were fortunate that someone lived to tell us what happened to my brother Leible.

VII

The Pascal Sacrifice

That spring of 1941 in the Skarzysko ghetto the last bits of snow melted from the street corners, and the sun shone brightly. April warmed the hearts of the people giving them strength from the spiritual and physical spring cleaning for Passover. The holiday spirit was in the air, and the streets of the ghetto were bustling. The black market was the only way in these difficult times to get what was needed.

The main problem was food, and the most scarce and precious holiday item was meat. Obtaining contraband meat in the ghetto was a major operation. First, the cow had to be smuggled into the ghetto by a Polish farmer at the risk of his life. The Jewish butcher who bought the cow was also in great danger. The greatest risk was taken by the shoichet who could be punished by death if caught performing ritual slaughter.

A couple of days before the holiday, Moishe the butcher confided to my father that an animal had been smuggled into the ghetto. My father was in charge of the slaughtering. Discovery at any stage by a German, Pole or the wrong Jew could mean death for all involved.

Moishe set the rendezvous for one o'clock when the German authorities were busy with lunch. The cow was hidden in the cellar which could only be entered through the kitchen. Father was anxious to get the dangerous operation over with as soon as possible, nervously insisting that I carry the knife in a long, narrow sheath on my back. Mother advised me to place a big scarf on my shoulder to cover the knife. After concealing the knife, I closely followed my father.

Before entering Moishe's place, I carefully handed Father the knife praying that God should watch over us. Moishe's son was also standing outside on the corner; he was our lookout.

The slaughtering normally took only a short time, but in those tense minutes of waiting I felt that something had gone wrong. Suddenly, two Polish policemen appeared and began looking up at the house. It seems they were tipped off. Moishe's son ran to warn his father of the danger. I went in through the back entrance. My father was standing by an open window. He had seen the police approach and had run up the stairs. He was now going to jump out the back window. He threw the knife down, which I grabbed as it fell to the ground. Then I watched as Father swung himself out of the window and desperately sought to hang on to the bricks jutting out of the wall. The police had entered the house by this time and as I bit my finger in fear, Father leaped from his precarious position. We narrowly avoided capture. The police had discovered and were examining the slaughtered animal, but miraculously we had enough time to escape.

After his jump, Father could hardly get up. At first, I feared he had broken a bone. With no time to lose, he forced himself to stand up and move as quickly as possible. Fortunately, my father was in good physical condition for a man in his late forties.

I half dragged Father to Aunt Hinda's who lived a few blocks away. Father was frightened both for himself and for my aunt, who was endangering herself by harboring him.

She applied cold compresses to his badly bruised knee and arm. My father's voice was full of grief as he spoke of poor Moishe the butcher who, at best, would lose his meager financial resources. He was also concerned about all the poor people who would have no meat to celebrate Passover.

I reminded him that we had enough matzah and potatoes to keep our stomachs from grumbling over Passover. I added that we should be grateful that at least we would be together. I then left Father with Aunt Hinda and returned home to take care of Mother, who still suffered tremendously from her heart condition. I had to assure her that everything was all right.

Father spent the next two days recuperating at Aunt Hinda's before returning home. Mother was so happy to see him, and we all thanked God for bringing him safely back to us. I extended my prayer, asking that he should be spared for as long as I lived.

Mother and I were preparing for our meager Passover meals when Aunt Hinda surprised us with a live chicken bought from a Polish farmer for a large sum of money. This rare luxury made our Passover very festive. The sight of my precious father at the head of the table filled my heart with love, but I knew we were not yet out of the woods.

With each passing day, I continued to fear that my father was still in danger from the Polish police and the constant German arrests and roundups. Father was in good spirits though feeling that God had spared his life so that he could be home for Passover with his family. Father never seemed to worry; he left his fate in the hands of God.

Two weeks later, after the holidays had ended, two Polish policemen suddenly entered our house with a warrant for Father's arrest. Father wasn't home at the time; he was visiting his friend Joseph. The police left the warrant, ordering my father to appear at the German headquarters as soon as he returned home. A new horror was upon us. Father had to hide and Mother could hardly stop crying. Another warrant followed the first; this one stating that any family member could take Father's place to offer information regarding the incident of the unauthorized slaughter. I decided to take the place of my father. I was scared, but I had no choice. I had to try anything to free my father. The night before I was due to stand before the German authorities, I couldn't sleep. Instead, I rehearsed the German words I would need to answer the charges. When morning arrived, I was terribly nervous. Mother's eyes were wide with fear, but I assured her there was nothing to worry about. After all, it was just a month before my seventeenth birthday. I was old enough to stand trial. Mother wished me luck and bade me a safe return.

It was eleven o'clock, the time of my appointment, when I arrived at the Gestapo headquarters. Two policemen stood guard on either side of the door. I tried not to tremble as I held the warrant in my hand and was ushered into the office. There at the front desk sat two officers in friendly conversation. Their smiling faces gave me a little courage, and I was able to speak clearly. One of the officers looked at the warrant and asked me where my father was hiding. I told him that we had received no word from Father in weeks. When he asked me if Father had slaughtered the animal, I swore that my father was innocent.

The officer warned me that if I was lying, I would be severely punished. I was old enough to be sent away to prison, which would mean certain death.

I looked straight into his eyes and again swore that my father was innocent. Tears covered my face, but I didn't even feel them as they dripped onto my trembling hands. Then the two officers looked at each other, a glance of pity passing between them. One of them signed the warrant which stated that Father was innocent of the charges and that his daughter had offered sworn testimony.

I took a closer step toward them and thanked them over and over. After the officer read the warrant for me in German, I went straight home to my Aunt Hinda's place where Father was hiding. I embraced my father and kissed him. "You are safe," I declared. "Let's go home and be together forever."

VIII

Pharoah in Jackboots

The ghetto became an increasingly impossible place to live. The shortage of food made life seem hopeless. Anti-Semitic violence raged on a daily basis. Young men were regularly taken away for forced labor.

My brother Zisman tried to keep up his optimism. But his dream faded away after he became an eye witness to the brutality of our Nazi oppressors.

By 1941 there was a great deal of construction going on under the direction of the Germans. Our region of Poland was known for its industry, especially its ammunition factories. So the Germans set up their work camps here. The problem was to find workers. Many of the skilled Polish laborers had been shipped off to work in German factories. Those who resisted working for the Nazis were either jailed or shot. So a few hundred Jews were recruited for the job.

My brother Zisman, along with many of the young men from Skarzysko, was forced to work clearing forest for the construction site of a new ammunition factory. What none of us knew at the time was that our men were also preparing what would become the camp in which Tobcia, Shmulek and I would be imprisoned.

Zisman was forced to cut down trees and dig. It was difficult, back-breaking work, especially for men unaccustomed to manual labor. Every day Zisman brought home terrible stories of torture and abuse. The S.S. treated Jews worse than animals because they were far more expendable.

If one slave-Jew collapsed the Germans knew they could lay their hands on another hundred to take his place. The Germans drove their slaves until they dropped, and the Ukrainian supervisors were even worse. Though the walk to and from the site was long, Zisman felt fortunate to be living at home. He could see that those living at the barracks were near death. Those unable to work there were immediately shot to be buried right there by their fellow workers.

The Sabbath proved particularly difficult for Zisman. Being Orthodox, he would not work on Saturdays. He found someone to work in his place and paid one of the Polish guards to overlook this replacement. Though the week was grueling, Zisman was happy to be able to fulfill his religious obligation and celebrate the Sabbath in peace.

One Sabbath, after he had been working at the construction site for eight months, Zisman and Father joined a prayer group that met at a friend's house. A patrol of German and Ukrainian police were then searching the neighborhood for able-bodied Jewish men. This patrol, accompanied by several members of the Jewish Committee, entered the ersatz synagogue where Zisman and Father were praying and immediately put the young men under arrest. Zisman took advantage of the initial commotion and slipped out the back door. His plan was to run home, change into his work clothes and return to the work site before anyone realized he was missing.

Unfortunately, the Jewish Committee representatives were forced to reveal the names of all the escapees, and by Sunday the police were at our door arresting my brother.

Zisman was in jail for three days. My parents worked tirelessly to gain the release of their beloved son. It was useless. On the fourth day we were notified by some members of the Jewish Committee that Zisman was granted a family "visit" before being taken off to a concentration camp. Zisman stood in the back of a wagon driven by two Poles. The wagon passed by our home slowly. I remained speechless while everyone around me was calling to him telling him not to give up. His eyes expressed much anger and sadness as he answered them, "Do not worry. I will be home soon. They will not get away with this." And then the wagon drove off.

Our house felt empty without my brother. We were terribly worried about him, and we all missed his smile, his high spirits and his wonderful stories. I was concerned for my mother's failing health. It was painful to see Mama gather my brother's clothes from the closet, wrap them around her head and weep. When she finally finished crying, she gazed upward and begged God to return her son to her.

Summer lapsed into fall. By November I found myself besieged by grief. My father's undying faith in God helped relieve his suffering, but mother mourned for her two beloved sons night and day. With tears rolling down her cheek. she often grasped a prayer book to her heart, pleading for God's mercy and protection.

My aunt and uncle tried to console my parents, but they could not convince them their sons would survive. In our hearts we knew the terrible truth, but we Jewish people are addicted to hope. We persist in believing that God will perform a miracle and save His children from destruction. My brothers, I thought, deserved such divine intervention. Were these not Biblical times as awesome as the slavery in Egypt? Both brothers were devoted to their parents and dedicated to the teachings of the Torah and Talmud. Surely they deserved to walk out alive from the lion's den and back into our empty home.

With the house enveloped in mourning, the only peaceful place to be was outside in the yard. There I could escape everything. I would dream that I was reunited with my brothers, sisters and best friends and that the war was finally over. The dream, though, would vanish quickly into our waking nightmare.

One day a mailman approached me even though it was forbidden to exchange letters with relatives. He handed me a postcard requesting twenty-five zlotys, approximately ten dollars, for the ashes of my brother Zisman's remains. Still clutching the postcard, I read those words from the authorities of Auschwitz over and over again. I was too shocked to feel anything, and, finally, I tore the card into little pieces. I remained calm, wiped my dry tears and went into the house.

Twenty-three-year-old Zisman was really gone and so were my hopes, my dreams, my faith.

The bitter winter of 1942 finally disappeared with its frost. The beauty and warmth of spring took its place, and once again the holiday of Passover was upon us. It was to be the last holiday I would celebrate with my family at home.

The last Seder was a painful reminder of so many things we had begun to take for granted before the war. As always, my father, the head of the household, sat with a pillow at his back. According to tradition, the pillow symbolized freedom, as only a free man could recline luxuriously at dinner. This ritual was especially meaningful as freedom had ceased to exist for us. Family is the core of Jewish life, and we had to face the fact that our family was slowly being eliminated. My mother sobbed to see the empty seats at the table.

My heart sank as I thought of my missing brothers. I listened to my father who said, "Passover teaches us never to give up hope. There must be some purpose for our suffering. Like our forefathers who went from bondage to freedom, we too shall emerge. We too are being purged and forged in a terrible crucible, but there will be a great redemption for our people."

My beloved aunt and uncle joined us around the Passover table. My aunt dared to get pregnant, for she yearned to have a child to replace the one she had lost. She prayed that God would help bring the baby into a better world. But the biggest miracle we prayed for was to have Moses reappear and lead the Jews of Europe into the promised land of Palestine.

I knew there was no "Next Year in Jerusalem" for my brothers. I thought about the ashen post card from Auschwitz. With those terrifying thoughts in my head I fell asleep and somehow dreamt of previous, joyous Passover holidays. My family prepared weeks in advance. Every inch of the house scrubbed until it smelled like roses. The dishes shimmering like diamonds and the kitchen smelling like a bakery. The tables were decked with traditional Passover foods as my father took my five brothers to shul. But, as usual, the dreams faded into scenes of the ghetto peopled by hunger, fear and the treading jack boots of the Angel of Death.

My parents helped me maintain my struggle to persevere. Mother's words gave me reason to believe: "As long as we have our health we can hope to survive until happier times." And Father spoke with his usual optimism when he promised that President Roosevelt would never let the Polish people down.

Around the middle of June, in 1942, rumors began to spread about our complete evacuation. In other parts of the city, many people had already been deported. Town meetings were held in our house to discuss our fears. We came to the conclusion that since there was nothing we could do, we must place ourselves in God's hands.

The orders soon followed. The Judenrat announced to the entire ghetto that the German commandant had ordered all Jewish girls between the ages of sixteen and eighteen to volunteer for a work camp. Only with our cooperation, we were told, would Skarzysko, be saved from complete evacuation. My friends and I were asked by the committee to register freely, hoping that the Germans would keep their word.

Though the fate of the entire ghetto rested on us, we "volunteers" were no heroes. My heart pounded with doubts. I was leaving a sick mother with a heart condition. I was the only girl at home. Only my two brothers, Moishe and Shmulek, would be left to care for Mama. My parents desperately wanted me to stay with them, but they wanted me to stay alive even more. Arrest and worse awaited those girls who did not "volunteer."

I registered. It would have been wonderful to have enjoyed the bright sun of that July day. Instead, the magnificent blue sky only emphasized the blackness inside our house. We were all overcome with sadness. It was to be my last night with my dear parents and brothers. How could I leave them?

The night was long, and sleep was impossible. I kept thinking that perhaps I would wake up to a miracle. The whole sleepless night I drove myself into a frenzy debating whether or not I should leave.

The next morning my parents saw how troubled and frightened I was. My face gave away my feelings. My father embraced me trying to comfort us both.

"My dear child," he said. "You have nothing to lose. If we will be spared because of your deeds, then you will be our savior. On the other hand, whatever comes of us, you may have a chance to survive if you are off working." He also reminded me that while I was away, I must try to keep my promise to be on my best behavior. "You were taught in religious school that everything happens for a reason. So go, my child. God is everywhere — He will be with you."

Finally at one o'clock in the afternoon, the signal came for the girls to leave. I looked at the simple iron bed where my father was resting. My mother was busy tying my clothes into a bundle so that I could hold onto them more easily. The tears kept rolling down her cheeks. My father, deep in thought, stood up. I looked at him and noticed how he had changed. His eyes grew dim as he embraced me and blessed me. "God should be with you," was all he said. My mother walked with me to the place where the girls were to assemble. She was still crying and could hardly speak, but I remember her whispering, "Perhaps a miracle will happen and you will come home soon."

My mother told me to take care of myself and to keep myself clean. "Yes, clean," I thought as my head was pounding and I felt dizzy from exhaustion. There were already about fifty girls gathered. They were sitting on their bundles, surrounded by S.S. men with rifles. A shiver went through my body as one of these men stopped my mother, telling her she could go no farther with me. I was too frightened to embrace her, and I bit my lip to keep from crying. That was the most horrible moment in my life — seeing the sadness in my mother's wet eyes. She threw me a kiss and walked away without a backward glance. Her body seemed twisted, and I'll never forget her shadowy figure in the distance. She turned into mist as she disappeared from my sight.

I wondered how I would manage to survive. Would I ever see my parents again? I sat on my bundle stealing glances at the other girls. After two hours of being assembled in the suffocating heat, our journey began. The S.S. forbade us to talk to each other. We were forced to walk faster and faster to our destination two miles away. I tried to look around. On either side of the road there were houses with pretty gardens. Polish people passed by. How I envied their freedom! At last we saw a sign that read "Arbeit Lager for Juden Hasak" (Hasak Work Camp for Jews). Together we entered the gates of Hell.

IX

Camp Hasak

The Hasak Camp near Skarzysko was huge, divided into three sections, and surrounded by barbed wire. Section A, where I was sent, was the biggest with about ten thousand inmates. The lager had a constant influx of new arrivals, most of whom had been forcibly brought from the shrinking ghettos of Warsaw, Lodz, and Krakow.

Six months in Camp Hasak was a lifetime for many of the prisoners. Conditions were unbearable, and selections occurred from once a week to once a month. As soon as a new group arrived, a selection was made to eliminate the weakest prisoners.

When we first arrived we were lined up five abreast and left to stand for hours under the blazing sun until the German commandant arrived. He was a short, ugly man named Kilermahn. As he looked us over, I wondered what he was thinking. How long would it take for us to turn into the faceless, lifeless skeletons we saw throughout the camp?

"You are in a work camp," the commandant began. "Understand that although you are not far from your homes, you might as well forget that they exist. You will not go home again. Whoever tries to run away will be shot. There will be no communication with your families."

After the speech, we were permitted to meet our fellow prisoners. We were surrounded by many familiar faces, inmates who had been brought to the camp weeks and months earlier. They were all eager to find relatives as they looked over the sad faces of the new "volunteers". I couldn't comprehend my new situation, and some inmates tried to cheer me up. They tried to relieve my stupor by telling me that we would all see the day of liberation. I envied their optimism.

I chose a top bunk. It wasn't the easiest to reach, but it was the cleanest. At least no straw or mud would fall in my face as I slept.

My body was limp with exhaustion. In the hot July weather, I stretched out on that top bunk, crying hysterically. My fellow inmates assured me that I would get used to it; they too had cried when they first arrived.

The first night was a nightmare. I was attacked by all kinds of insects. I couldn't fall asleep, and before I knew it, the morning alarm began to ring. All of us rose and stood in line for an hour before going to work.

We were then led to the big ammunition factory. There were many inmates there, both men and women. Our meisters, or supervisors, were Poles. Our work lasted from seven in the morning until six in the evening and was divided into a day shift and a night shift.

I wished I could sprout wings and fly home. I wondered if the people back in the ghetto knew what was going on. I bitterly recalled how I had been tricked into volunteering to leave home in order to save my parents. I couldn't forgive myself for not staying home — even in hiding. I wanted desperately to survive this ordeal and get back home.

While working at the machines, I talked to myself, praying that we would be freed. My Polish meister, unaware of my prayers, smiled each time he looked at me. He was satisfied to see this Jewish girl working so hard helping his section meet its quota. In return, he brought me news from the city. Each day he told me which towns had been cleaned out and made Judenrein. He was waiting for word of the evacuation of our city so he could loot the abandoned Jewish homes.

As difficult as things were, I knew I was better off than other inmates. For instance, most of those from Warsaw, Krakow or other big cities had come from ghettos that had been liquidated. The few women who had survived from these cities had no families praying for their return. Since the smaller cities were still relatively safe then, I lived with the hope that in a matter of time I would be free to go home.

Our food rations were terribly limited. We had no breakfast. We were given a bowl of soup for lunch and a piece of bread and some coffee made from corn for dinner. We would save half of this bread and eat it the next morning to help us get through the day. The food was almost impossible to subsist on.

One day I received a godsend in the form of a visit from my brother Moishe. I'll never forget my happiness when I was called to the gates by the guard. I wasn't permitted to talk to Moishe while the guard examined the food package. But we had time to read each other's thoughts and look into each other's eyes before he was ordered to leave.

I still remember Moishe standing before me — a handsome boy of sixteen with shining eyes and a soft smile who wanted to talk to me and tell me so much. Moishe was only eighteen months younger than I and we were as close as twins. He was tall and good looking with jet black eyes and black curly hair. He was a gentle boy who loved mathematics. He was never without a pencil doing math problems. His was one of many careers cut short by the Germans, but it was particularly sad to me. Aunt Hinda's husband, Rachmil, had found Moishe a job at the railway station where he used his privileges to bring me food from home.

Equal to the problem of keeping well-nourished was that of keeping clean. Many of us had no changes of clothes. It was also difficult to wash the clothes we wore.

We were given no privacy. There was one washroom for men, and another one for women. Each had only a few cold water spigots to be shared by several thousand inmates.

At night when I returned from the factory, I'd wash out my dress and hang it up to dry. I was one of the fortunate few who had two dresses and that rarest of commodities — a piece of soap. This soap saved my life because it allowed me to stay cleaner and fresher looking than other inmates, a crucial factor in the constant selections.

I also was fortunate to have a feather pillow and blanket which I had brought in with me. We had to keep any possessions with us, as even the smallest item was coveted by the inmates. After two years, the pillow and blanket were stiff from dirt, but I still appreciated them on winter nights.

In 1943, a shipment of clothes from Auschwitz and Treblinka was dispersed to the Hasak inmates. One woman ripped open the seams in a girdle she got and found a small diamond. The lucky inheritor of this smuggled diamond traded it to a Polish supervisor and ate extra portions of bread for several weeks.

X

Hanka

Of all the precious young girls who were incarcerated in our work camp during the war, one particular girl became my best friend. Her name was Hanka.

Hanka and her mother arrived at Skarzysko lager after I had been there for several weeks. Sent from Warsaw, they were assigned to my barracks.

Hanka's mother had a sophisticated look with her jet black hair pulled back in a chignon. She was a soft-spoken woman and had an excellent vocabulary in her native Polish. Her daughter Hanka was blond, with sky-blue eyes and straight hair. Just sixteen, she was greatly admired in our barracks for her beauty.

Mother and daughter were very close. For the first few days, Hanka's mother cried continuously despite Hanka's pleas to stop. The older woman kept wailing, "There are only the two of us! A few days ago we were a large family — where are they now? Will I ever see them again?" I was heartbroken for her, and her tears reopened my own fresh wounds.

As we became better acquainted, she began to relate her family's recent ordeal. Hanka, her mother and father, her twelve-year-old brother, her grandparents and an uncle were about to be deported from Warsaw several days earlier. The family expected group relocation, but the officials came and dragged the family to a truck, leaving only Hanka and her mother behind to watch in horror.

After a couple of weeks Hanka and her mother slowly adjusted to the cheerless and exhausting life in the work camp. They too were assigned to the ammunition factory to produce bullets for the German war effort — literally arming our enemies. After many long hours of this deadening routine, we shuffled back to our barracks for a meager supper.

The routine was shattered one morning when Hanka's mother refused to move from her bunk. Hanka panicked when she realized her mother was sick. The woman's face was white and her forehead burned with fever. She screamed that she couldn't stand the pain in her head.

Everyone wanted to help, but we were all too frightened to linger. We had to be out of the barracks by a certain time for the morning roll call. The twenty girls from our bunk house ended up running as fast as they could to avoid the harsh punishment for tardiness.

I lingered behind for a moment as Hanka continued to cry. She was the only girl in our barracks who had her mother with her. I could not help envying her, even while I could see the specter of death on her mother's face. It seemed such a tragedy. She was only in her late thirties. I recognized her deadly symptoms — it was the same typhus I had back in the ghetto.

I ran to put a wet compress on her forehead. Then I dragged Hanka with me to stand on apel (roll call). I assured her that her mother would be fine and told her not to worry. "It's probably the flu," I lied.

Hanka was restless all day, desperate to get back to her mother. But, meanwhile, her mother's condition had worsened. The block elster (warden) advised Hanka to take her mother to the nurse for help, but the intervention of camp authorities frightened Hanka even more.

When we got to her mother's side, Hanka began to shake. I tried to calm her while holding her mother up with my free arm. She could hardly stand, but with all her strength she tried to make it with us to the infirmary.

Hanka's mother looked up to the stars overhead and asked weakly, "What will they do to me? What help can I possibly get from them? I just feel like I'm going to collapse!" I assured her she would be all right.

"It's just a bad flu," I said.

"I've had many colds in my life," she responded grimly, "but I've never felt like this."

When we arrived at the medical barracks, the nurse appeared to be waiting for us. She was a cold woman, the hardened receptionist of the Angel of Death. After checking the patient's temperature, the nurse ordered Hanka and me back to our barracks. Hanka's mother was to be taken to the sick ward. The hospital was known to be the vestibule of hell, and I cried as mother and daughter embraced lovingly — perhaps for the last time. The nurse, herself a prisoner, again ordered us to leave, and so we made our tearful way back to the barracks.

When morning came, Hanka hardly spoke to me. Her face was hard and tight, a mortar shell ready to explode. At work, she couldn't even eat the precious little soup given to us for lunch. She lived only for the moment that she could return to camp and perhaps be permitted to see her mother.

I offered to go along with Hanka, and so, after receiving permission, we ran back to the ward. The same head nurse stood outside awaiting us. She stepped forward ominously and told Hanka that while we had been at work, a "selection" had taken place in camp. Her mother had been among those "selected."

Hanka stood still in shock. Then she let out a scream that could be heard throughout the camp. I desperately tried to get her to pull herself together. As I held onto her, she demanded that the nurse tell her where her mother had been taken. "I want to be with my mother," she pleaded.

"Your mother has been taken there," the nurse said sharply, pointing to the forest facing our camp. "All the prisoners who were selected were shot and buried in that forest."

Hanka cried and cried. She repeatedly asked, "Where is my mother? She was supposed to protect me!" At that point she lapsed into a near-daydream state. She was constantly lost in thought. Since losing her mother, she began to dwell more on the loss of the rest of the family. She couldn't cope with the weight of all the tragedy that had fallen upon her within so short a time.

I tried to console her, to tell her that she was not the only victim. We had all lost our precious families.

"We have to survive," I insisted. "We must tell the world."

"We will be the witnesses for all time!" I told her how every time I was angry about starvation in the ghetto, my father would say, "In time you will see, my darling daughter. Hitler will fall just like any other man. Have faith!"

But Hanka was not consoled by my words; she just stared at me. Hanka's mind was in a shallow grave with her family. Day after day I watched my friend deteriorate. She refused to wash her hair or clean her dress, although I begged her to do so. In just a few months, this beautiful young girl had become like a vegetable and had completely lost her will to live.

Most selections took place in the spring or autumn, when the forest soil was soft for digging. A selection was announced one beautiful morning in 1943. All the prisoners assembled for inspection by our oberfuhrer. Butenshlager was a tall, handsome monster dressed in an immaculate S.S. uniform. A huge German shepherd stood at his side as he studied the faces of each of the prisoners before him.

Our faces were frozen and emotionless; only our minds were working, wanting desperately to live. Hanka, who stood next to me, stiffened when the oberfuhrer pointed his finger at her and ordered her to step out.

How frantically I wanted to hold her close to me! Why did they have to kill this beautiful young girl, my only friend?

For the rest of my time in camp, I blinked back tears each time I looked at the forest. There were buried thousands of innocent young victims like Hanka and her mother — united in an unmarked grave in cursed Polish soil.

Rest in peace, Hanka. Who will visit your grave? The summer stars? The winter wind that moans in the forest for your tortured soul?

XI

Found and Lost

The bitter weeks passed. By the end of August, more transports arrived daily. Returning from work, I was eager to find out from where each new group had come. I kept hoping to find a relative or to meet someone with news of one. I also needed somebody to talk to with Hanka gone.

The High Holidays came, and I cried my heart out when I didn't hear from home. We had no communication with the outside world, except for an occasional word from my Polish meister about which ghettos were being evacuated. Each day I prayed, "Oh God — why don't you see how much we need a miracle?"

I will never forget that sad Yom Kippur Eve. Most of the inmates would not eat our meager slice of bread. These morsels were reserved for after the fast. All that day we worked, admiring each other's strength in keeping the fast. I remembered my family attending shul on this holy day and being impressed by the sight of so many people feeling faint from hunger — and then we had feasted the night before. Yet in Camp Hasak, with just one slice of bread the day before, we miraculously fasted and kept working for nearly two days.

Yom Kippur fell on the Sabbath that year, making it an exceptionally holy day. It became special to me for other reasons as well. Late in the afternoon, there was a commotion in the camp. A huge transport had arrived. I hungrily searched their faces and, sure enough, I found out that this group was from Suchedniow. I immediately rushed toward them to look for my sister Esther or her family.

Since she and her husband Joseph were in their early twenties, they were likely to be sent to a labor camp. I was searching the sea of faces when suddenly I heard a voice calling, "Miss Walshaw!" I jumped with excitement and spun around to see who it was.

It was my friend Joshua! A voice and face from happier times.

"I'm so happy to see you!" he exclaimed. I smiled and thought to myself, "Is this Joshua, the fellow I couldn't talk to back home? How my sister would tease me because I was too young for him!" Now, years later, Joshua stood before me again. I was grown up now, a young woman in my late teens. It was no longer necessary to hide the way I felt towards Josh. The war years and the concentration camp had closed the gap between us.

Joshua had only a few minutes before being taken away with the rest of the men. He told me about Esther, her husband, and their two little boys, who had been sent away to the crematorium with most of the others from the town of Suchedniow. Joshua had escaped death, but he was very lonely. We were parted by barking orders and shuffling columns, but were cheered by this mutual discovery.

It was already late. The stars had appeared, signalling the end of the Yom Kippur fast. I finished my dinner of stale bread and was overcome with bitterness weeping for my poor sister and her family — reduced to ashes and memories.

It was a great comfort to have Joshua nearby for two years. During that time we took every opportunity to meet. On Sundays, the men were allowed to visit relatives in the women's barracks. Joshua was a regular visitor. It was difficult for us to see each other under such circumstances — there was no privacy. We would sit and talk the afternoon away. At nightfall, when all visitors had to leave, I would walk Joshua as far as I could. When it was time to park, we would linger, not knowing what to say or do. Joshua was a young man, after all, with a young man's desires, and although I was still young and inexperienced, I had matured tremendously in that short time in camp. We both longed to plan a future together, yearning for love and warmth. We would stare into each other's eyes, trying to express this love, but knowing that we would have to wait. Our surroundings didn't dampen our passion, but it did make anything other than a goodbye kiss seem inappropriate.

Lovemaking was extremely dangerous. Even married couples risked severe punishment. If a woman became pregnant in camp, she was considered a traitor to the war effort and immediately executed.

Joshua and I knew that our love would have to remain within, and we both prayed for the time when we could fully share and express what was in our hearts.

Meanwhile, I could not put aside my grief over the loss of my sister and her family. At night I lay awake until the morning bell. My polish meister noticed how red my face had become from crying. I told him that the Suchedniow ghetto had been liquidated. He warned me to be prepared, for Skarzysko would be next. His words chilled me. I bit my lip and did not give him the satisfaction of showing emotion.

I suffered tremendously, only thinking about how I could escape and join my parents before the Germans came for them.

Succoth came to an end, and I lived with the hope that a miracle would occur before the next holiday, Simchat Torah.

The joyous celebration of renewal — Simchat Torah — came, but there would be no joy. That day, my meister didn't say his usual "good morning." The ammunition machines ran at full speed, but my heart seemed to race even faster. Something was going on.

About lunch time, my meister came over to tell me that the Skarzysko ghetto had been evacuated at eleven o'clock that morning. The only thing I could do was whisper, "Oh, my God." I sobbed my heart out, unable to forgive myself for not having managed to escape. For six weeks I had thought only about being with my parents. But it was useless. I was imprisoned in a concentration camp. I didn't think I could last much longer. My head was spinning. I believed that my life, too, would shortly come to an end.

I prayed in my own way to God — but where was He? The answer came when Simchat Torah was over. The bell rang; the machines groaned to a full stop. Marching back to the camp with our heads down, I noticed that a new transport of people had arrived. When I found out that they were from our city, I could hardly wait to be released from apel.

Suddenly, as if in a dream from heaven, I heard a loud voice screaming, "Rachela!" But who could it be? My parents, in their late forties, were not young enough to have been brought here to work. My youngest brother, Shmulek, was a mere child. As for the rest of the family, they had already vanished.

Eagerly scanning the rows, I saw my sister Tobcia stretching out her arms to me. Momentarily paralyzed, I couldn't believe that I had been reunited with my sister.

Our emotion-clogged throats finally loosened. I asked her how she had come to be a part of that transport group. She explained that Szydloviec, where she had been living, had been evacuated two weeks before. But that was all she could say.

Being together after so long was overwhelming. Soon our inhibitions were gone and we tearfully embraced. I finally brought myself to ask about Tobcia's husband and her two little girls, Rachel and Chayah. My sister bit her finger.

"Don't cry," she said. Shmulek is also here — he was taken to Werk C. I am alone."

I understood what she meant. Her family was gone, and I dared not question her further. She had been through enough. Just looking at her face, I could see how much she had changed. How wild and bitter she had become.

The first night sleeping beside my sister, I tossed and turned wondering how she would respond to the misery she would encounter here. I watched her as she slept. Even in slumber, she looked strained, exhausted. How could she look otherwise? How could a mother lose her children and go on living?

Tobcia and her husband Sharie had lived in the Jewish community of Szydloviec with their two little girls, Rachel and Chaya. Before the Jewish holidays, news of cruel actions and attacks on many ghettos had spread rapidly to Szydloviec. Most of the victims were to vanish in the death camps of Treblinka, while a handful would be sent to established concentration camps. The holy day of Yom Kippur was chosen by the Nazis as a fitting time to "clean up" the Jewish ghettos, once and for all.

Physically and psychologically beaten by years of oppression, many Jews went like weary sheep to their deaths. My brother-in-law and my sister, however, were determined to survive. They carefully planned a hiding place and built a bunker in the basement of their house.

When the mass deportation started, they suffered a last-minute panic. Should they hide alone or join the fate of their community? The "safety in numbers" instinct was strong, even when the "numbers" were adding up to six million. But the will to live was stronger than any herd instinct; they wanted desperately to stay alive!

For two weeks they hid in the bunker — truly a living hell. Their first day was spent fighting off the rats who smelled their human flesh. Tobcia and Sharie took turns staying awake to keep the rodents off their children. Huddled fearfully beneath their own house, they heard everything that went on above. After the lions, the vultures; after the Germans, the Poles. They heard their Polish neighbors entering their home and moving out all their furniture and belongings. For five days, they listened to the sound of all they had worked for being carted away.

And then it was quiet. All the Jews were evacuated. The ghetto was as deserted as a graveyard. The only Jews left were the few in hiding, like Tobcia and her family. Surrender was inevitable, for there was no way to escape. Food and water had soon run out,

My sister's young children somehow understood. They suffered in silence, never crying out nor asking for food and water. The family could only whisper, clutching desperately to their love of life. They had no alternative.

Tobcia and Sharie made up their minds to come out of hiding and leave the bunker. At first, the daylight was blinding, having been underground for two weeks. Sharie decided to try the Poles whom they had entrusted with some of their goods. Sharie was about to ask for a few scraps of bread for their children.

"I will go out first with Rachela," he instructed Tobcia. "You stay behind the gate with the little one. Wait a few minutes before following me so I can see if the street is clear of Germans. In case you hear something, I want you to go back to the bunker immediately. Maybe you'll have a better chance if you wait there."

She held onto him, pleading to go outside together. But he refused, closing the gate and leaving her behind.

Standing a block behind with her little child in her arms, she heard a loud voice demanding, "Stop! Are you a Jew?"

"Yes," she heard Sharie reply.

Just one bullet did the job.

Tobcia clamped her hand over the child's mouth to stifle her cry. Then she returned, shaken, to the bunker. Only her husband's final wishes kept her alive.

Tobcia could scarcely wait until the morning to surrender to the S.S. She thought of taking her own life, but could not bear the thought of abandoning her baby. As she sat unable to sleep, she talked to herself and begged God for mercy.

Suddenly, she thought she heard a cat mewing. Listening carefully, she realized that it didn't sound like a cat at all, but rather like a child crying. She lifted the opening to the kitchen, and saw her little Rachel trying to find her way back.

The child's head had been injured. Lying next to her father, Rachel had remained still, playing dead until she saw the S.S. man leave. When she touched her father and he did not respond, she tried to get back to the family's hiding place. At the age of six, little Rachel had found a way to survive.

Rachel's head was covered with blood. Tobcia tore a sheet and cleaned her child's head, but she could not relieve Rachel's fever. No one can describe the misery my sister went through that night.

Finally, Tobcia joined a handful of others who had also tried to hide, but now had to give themselves up. A Polish nurse bandaged Rachel's head. My sister was relieved to learn that they were to be sent back to Skarzysko. My parents informed her that Esther and her two infant sons had been deported.

After a family meeting, my brother Moishe gathered together a few valuables and put them into a heavy glass jar that was buried in the ground. Even at this stage the family had hopes for a time after the war when they could return to claim our goods and start a new life.

On October 3, 1942, the evacuation of Skarzysko began. Tobcia's family reunion was only to last one night. Very early that morning all were roused by voices shouting, "Everybody out! Everybody out!" People were running and screaming; crying children were trying to find their parents. The Germans were beating people with their rifle butts. When they were satisfied that all the houses were empty, the Nazis gathered everyone together in a field and made them stand in rows to be counted. Next to my family was a pregnant woman who was crying because she had lost one of her children. A German soldier told her to be still, but she carried on her search. The soldier shot her dead.

Soon, a large group of camp inmates were brought in to join the Skarzysko evacuees in the selection field. They were already half dead and their faces were yellow from working, unprotected, with gun powder. It was then that everyone began to suspect that they were headed to a death camp, rather than a labor camp.

Father covered himself in his prayer shawl and prayed.

Eventually, they started selecting healthy, young men and women between the ages of sixteen and thirty. Tobcia was sent to join the group bound for the work camp. Shmulek was not chosen as he was yet too small.

Leaving her children was the most difficult thing Tobcia had ever done. She was struck several times on the head while her little ones clung to her. All she could manage to say was, "Mama, take care of the children!" She would never see her parents or children again.

XII

Siblings in Barbed Wire

Because of his job, Moishe was not evacuated with the family. He and about fifty other railway workers remained behind to clean up the ghetto. My brother Shmulek, then, was the only son left to stand with our parents before they were taken off to the death camp. That he escaped the same fate at the last moment was just an accident. I'd use the word "miracle," but it seems so inappropriate for these god-forsaken times.

As they stood waiting to board the deportation wagon, my mother whispered to Shmulek to run and join Tobcia. Father was still rendering his farewell prayer at the time. Without thinking, Shmulek ran across the field and hid behind Tobcia. He hadn't even said goodbye.

A commotion arose among the crowd of people. A Jewish policeman and an S.S. officer were asking for volunteers to stay behind and join the railway workers in cleaning up the ghetto. There were not enough volunteers so more had to be chosen. Shmulek was frightened that he would be discovered, but somehow he was overlooked and taken with Tobcia to Camp Hasak.

Those who remained behind in Skarzysko met a sad end. In December of 1942, typhoid broke out in the ghetto, and all were sent to their deaths.

Shmulek was at first assigned to Werk A. I was delighted to have my brother nearby, although I couldn't communicate with him. Once a week, those in his sector were brought to mine to take showers, and I could see him for a short time. Unfortunately, because of his size and age, he was one of the lower grade workers transferred to Werk C.

It was not long before he was barely recognizable, as his sector, Werk C, offered inmates the harshest conditions. He was assigned to Pikrina, the gunpowder detail, where only a handful survived. Being a clever young boy, Shmulek immediately concluded that he had to find a way out. Turning yellow from the toxic chemicals was as good as a death sentence.

He got together with a young man named Abraham and together they made up their minds to run away. They planned to hide in the woods, hoping to find some partisans willing to help them escape. The risks involved were terrifying, yet there seemed to be no alternative.

They waited for the right moment and managed to cross over the barbed wire fences. The two desperate youngsters had no provisions and no friend, but they had escaped the campgrounds. Just as they were about to breathe a sigh of relief, they were spotted.

In his mind, Shmulek became a bird floating through empty space. He recalled the sensation of moving his legs without moving. The reverie was broken by gunshots and bullets whizzing around him. Abraham dropped behind while Shmulek plunged into a river and swam his way through the frigid waters to safety. He found his way back to the ghetto but quickly realized that it was too dangerous to stay. His only thought was to return to the relative safety of Werk A.

And so he headed back to our concentration camp. It was a big risk for a Jewish boy who could easily be recognized as a former camp prisoner. Shmulek reached his destination and was immediately arrested by the Jewish Police. Shmulek's history at Hasek was easy to figure out due to his yellowed face. The police were amazed that he had managed to escape Werk C, but they held him chained in miserable circumstances until a German officer came to determine his fate.

By this time word had reached us of the young escapee from Werk C in police custody. Tobcia and I went to our Jewish lager fuhrer, Her Albert, to plead our brother's case.

Herr Albert from Skarzysko called me into his office and explained Shmulek's predicament to me with a certain degree of sensitivity. He knew us well from home.

I pleaded with Herr Albert to let me speak to my brother Shmulek. Not only did he grant my request, but he advised me to tell Shmulek that his only chance rested upon getting an interview with Lager Fuhrer Kilermahn of the S.S. During this interview he must say that he had run away only to be with his sisters in Werk A.

The interview was arranged and my brother Shmulek was assigned to work with me. Werk A laborers made shells for bullets used in machine guns and other ammunition. To produce the shell took approximately fifteen operations. Our specific job was to imprint the shell's stamp of origin and, at the same time, to punch a hole where the firing pin had to engage. Shmulek was a good worker and was soon promoted to a machine setter in charge of three units. A girl was stationed at each machine, and I was one of those girls. I was relieved that the three of us were finally together, amazed at the close call we had all suffered through.

Shmulek became somewhat of a local hero, being the only person to escape Werk C and live to tell about it.

Our first bitter winter in the camp was upon us. We spent hours before and after each day's work, standing and shivering in the frozen snow. We had few clothes, and with each passing day I became more and more desperate to get back to my bunk and devour my rationed slice of bread.

My sister Tobcia and I worked on opposite shifts. While I was going to work, she was returning. We usually took strength on being together on Sundays, but sometimes even that was difficult for me.

I remember one Sunday, as we were discussing our plight, Tobcia suddenly covered her face with her hands and began to sob. She spoke about her children, how desperately she missed them. I tried to ease her sorrow by telling her that she was not the only one going through these hard times. There were so many others all around us who had lost their own precious ones. When I realized what I was saying, I was overcome with guilt and begged my sister to forgive me. I had meant to relieve her pain, but how could I hope to do so? She often had said to me, "You don't understand what it means to be a mother, to lose children." She was right. I couldn't possibly understand.

We each had our share of grief. For a time I found the time and place to cry at work. While I toiled, my mind raced in different directions. I often fantasized that I would see my family again.

After a while, I stopped crying. I had no tears left. I felt myself beginning to prepare for my death. As I watched so many weakening and vanishing around me, what choice did I have?

Each day I looked around me, nothing more who were missing. They had been so young and healthy, held so precious by their parents, and now they were buried in the forest facing our barracks. Thousands lay there, some buried alive in that one vast, unmarked grave. When would it be my turn? Who would be left to cry for me?

Sunday was a busy day. The weekly cleaning of my hair and dress was an experience which I looked forward to all week, one which helped make the days pass more quickly. On Sundays, too, I met Joshua. We were always delighted to see each other. Despite the rough existence in the camp, he tried to keep up his appearance. He was a good-looking fellow, and he reminded me of my happy teenage years when I stayed with my sister Esther and eagerly vied for his attention. I was also happy to see that my sister felt comfortable with Joshua. Joshua and Tobcia were intelligent and informed young people who found a lot to talk about. I was delighted that she had found someone who could understand her — someone with whom she could share her thoughts.

During this time, my primary concern was to keep from getting sick. I often saw my fellow inmates removed from our group after failing health. The commanders kept a lookout for those who looked pale or worn out. I soon learned to stand straight and pinch my cheeks to look healthy. Despite my precautions, my heart raced each time the oberfuhrer looked into my eyes.

Many times I actually was sick. I felt my lips burning with fever, but I was afraid to stay in the bunk or to fall behind in my work. At roll call I stood up and forced myself not to fall. The most dangerous illness was typhus. It had been a blessing in disguise that Shmulek and I had already had this disease in the ghetto and were now immune. Had we come down with typhus while in captivity, we would have surely perished.

I will never forget when an inmate I was friendly with was struck with typhus. Because of my immunity I was permitted to visit her. It is nearly impossible to fully describe the way in which the camp's typhus victims were forced to live.

The ward was long and narrow, men and women divided on each side. As I stood staring helplessly, they were all moaning pitifully. They lay on wooden pallets, naked under pieces of paper.

I walked over to the woman who had been my friend. She hardly opened her eyes. Her beautiful blonde hair was infested with lice. It was useless to speak to her; she could not respond. She was better off dead; even the quick agony of the gas chamber was preferable to suffering like this.

My mind begins to race. I can no longer stifle my thoughts, my guilt, the dreadful images and memories. The truck comes to take the typhus victims from the ward. Some of them have mercifully died, but many are to be buried alive. I am still alive — but I am buried alive. Buried in the painful past, under a forest of rooted memories.

The month of March, 1943, was especially horrible. The piles of snow had started to melt and my feet became soaked in the deep, soft snow while standing on apel twice a day. My shoes filled with mud and water. Life was unbearably harsh due to the hunger and cold.

After work I slowly chewed my precious little portion of bread and then tried to sleep. The snow melting on the wooden roof seeped though the wooden slats, however, and often fell on me. I had to shift from place to place to avoid the dripping ice water. The nights were so miserable that I was happy to hear the morning bell ring. I wouldn't even mind standing on apel in the frigid cold again. I was eager to get to work where at least there was adequate shelter. We had heat from the lights and the machines, and the work itself wasn't bad.

The night shifts were the most difficult. I couldn't sleep in the barracks during the day because of the noise from other inmates. Working made the night seem so long, I thought the day would never come. Listening to the monotonous sounds of the huge machines lulled me to sleep many times, and I was awakened by a sharp slap in the face from the commander. He hit me so hard that I thought my teeth would fall out.

My life was hectic either way, day or night shift. Each was its own hell to live through. My work now consisted of producing bullets and checking them for quality control. Many times I was alerted by other inmates when the controller was coming. I would panic and check the materials many times. I was often beaten and I feared for my life. Doing faulty work was considered sabotage. Each time the controller tested the bullets, I felt my heart beating faster and my body sinking.

But soon I became numb to this pressure, too. I stopped caring about anything. I was prepared for the end. After all, why should my fate be different from anyone else's? I was deeply depressed. I felt the gaping vacuum of my missing family. I often contemplated their final painful hours. I wore pessimism like ashes on my head. I could see no roads beyond the camp and the beckoning forest of corpses. Life had become too difficult to hold any meaning for me.

I had become accustomed to a life that smelled of death. I was used to seeing inmates wrapped in rags. The most cultured and refined of inmates would have to humble themselves to the lowest to get a little more soup. Once proud people had to grapple in the dust for a half ladle of broth that had spilled on the ground. They would pick it up with their hands and put it right into their mouths. The hunger reduced humans into animals.

On our way back from work, we would often see a Polish man with a tag on his chest hanging by a rope at the front gate. These men were being punished for stealing ammunition. But even this grisly sight did not disturb me anymore. After two years, I had become numb.

Pulling me through to the land of the living was my sister Tobcia. She was like a mother to me, encouraging me to go on, to stay alive.

"You should be stronger than me," she often said to me. "Look what I lost! But after all, we must live. We must live to take revenge and tell our people what we went through." Her spirit gave me hope, blowing pathways through the clouds of my depression.

XIII

Waltzing with the Angel of Death

I became so run down that I was struck with dysentery. I thought it was all over. The pain in my stomach was indescribable. I vomited for three days, lying on my bunk. I could hardly wait for my sister to come from work each day to help me get a little warm water.

Staying away from work or failing to appear on *apel* was risky, but luckily my supervisor at the factory was kind.

Rutka saved my life by convincing the meister that I was temporarily unable to leave the bunk for a few days. As soon as I could, I rushed back to work to confirm my productivity, my license to exist.

After a few weeks, however, I became sick again. I couldn't pass urine. I fainted from pain each time I went to the latrine. When I told my sister about my condition, she was worried and tried to help. I walked around for days with terrible pain, until I passed out in the barracks. I had a high fever and could only see shadows. I felt as if my body were floating in the air. I lay sick with fever for ten days, unable to urinate. I was not even conscious of what was happening to me.

Thanks to my friend Rutka I was able to cover up. She was the one who counted the workers and reported the missing — in return for extra soup and bread.

On the seventh and worst night of my illness I cried myself to sleep. Suddenly, my mother appeared in the barracks, looking beautiful. She was wearing lipstick, which

I had never seen her wear before, and carrying a bunch of colorful flowers.

"Mother," I cried with arms extended, "talk to me." But even in my dream I realized that she was not alive. She approached and gave me her flowers, half of which spilled out on the ground. I bent down to pick them up, and when I got up Mother was gone.

Just then Tobcia returned from work and I felt her cool hand on my burning forehead. When I told her of my vision she said that I would now recover, that Mother came to give me health.

My temperature dropped by the hour, my vision cleared, and I was finally able to pass water. The urine was black as ink.

This waltz with the Angel of Death helped me recover my will to live. With the help of my sister and friends, my strength eventually returned. It was so difficult to return to work, but the inmates were happy to see me on my feet again. Few thought that I would survive.

Pulling myself together, I borrowed some rouge and, with trembling fingers, painted some health on my face. I was somehow able to hide my weak condition from my meister and to survive a selection that Sunday conducted by the SS monster Buttenshlagen. Rutka encouraged me at work, and my brother Shmulek checked on the quality of my bullet production. I soon appreciated being alive.

Spring weather was approaching, and the Germans started to clean up the winter's mess. I watched the supreme kapos remove skeletons from the wooden trunk where they had been stored all winter like frozen sardines. They were loaded onto trucks bound for a forest burial. Such grisly sights no longer frightened us. We were concerned only with survival, like animals.

A few dim rays of light stole their way into this crude, dark existence. My sister Tobcia lent me a share of her strength and courage while Joshua and my brother visited more often. Rumors were circulating that the Germans were losing the war and this news gave us renewed passion for life.

My sister assured me that we would see the collapse of Germany, and I did notice the changes in the Hasak work camp. Some of the German meisters were reassigned and there was fear on the faces of those remaining — though not enough to suit us.

Many inmates talked of escape, but the armed presence of the Germans was still too strong. Hope and hopelessness kept colliding. Even though the situation seemed to be changing, it was difficult to believe that we might live to see the collapse of the Germans. It was impossible to hope that they would allow us to survive to witness their defeat.

Nevertheless, by mid August, 1944, the sun was bright and the air was full of hope. The Russians were rumored to be near. We were merely stationed in the barracks then, as no more work was being done. All the valuable machines were being taken apart and sent back to Germany. Many of the plant's German engineers left to return to their homeland. Our Polish workers brought news that Russia was very strong and would soon liberate Poland.

Still, there were mixed feelings in the camp. Some inmates remained pessimistic, believing that the Germans would butcher us before surrendering Poland. Even those who had faith in a military liberation were reluctant to chance a break-out. It seemed that we were being watched even more closely. With our rations and strength so low it was difficult to find the desire necessary for action. Passivity weighed us down as our skeletal bodies lost further weight.

After weeks of watching and waiting, news finally came. The kapo informed us that some of us would be transported to Leipzig, while others would be shifted to different parts of the Hasak complex. This made us suspicious and fearful.

A selection started. Many of the weak were taken away to be buried in the woods. The inmates in the sick ward were taken out first. They stared pathetically at us as they were pushed into the trucks.

Butenshlager paced back and forth, the cold monster who decided who among us would become fertilizer for the trees. That same evening the remaining inmates received half a loaf of bread and were told that the next day we were to be transferred to Germany. The day before my sister and I left for Leipzig, Shmulek and Joshua came to our barracks. Shmulek was confused and fearful about our separation. Although liberation seemed so close, there was still no reason to hope for survival.

As I looked at my little brother, my heart filled with fear. Would he be able to survive? We kissed each other and hoped for an eventual reunion. Joshua and I were too saddened to talk. Instead, we looked into each other's eyes. Finally, Joshua spoke.

"Who knows? The time may come for us to be together." He took my hand and held it against his chest, whispering, "If we survive, we will share our happiness together."

I then kissed him and he said, "Be brave. Have courage." We couldn't know that it was to be our last goodbye.

It was difficult to sleep that night. The morning arrived quickly, though, with the kapos running about wildly. Their orders were to get us out as swiftly as they could. There was no time to talk or say goodbye to the other inmates.

We were taken by truck to a train yard and then loaded onto cars. We were packed like sardines into a cattlecar and the stench was suffocating. The whole thing took days, but nobody died in our cars. Everyone aboard was strong enough to survive. We reached Germany and were taken to Leipzig for a new turn in our careers as slaves.

XIV

Taken to the Lions' Den

Leipzig, situated in Eastern Germany, was known throughout Europe for its culture and civilization. It was here in this fairyland city of light that we spent a dark summer in 1944.

Lepzig was also known for its munitions industry. We were brought to a camp only a mile from the factories. This meant more ammunition work. Soon after our arrival, we were standing on apel listening to a tall, husky lager fuhrer explain that our work would be similar to our assignment in Poland. He also informed us that we would work in proximity with German workers, but that it was absolutely forbidden to converse with them. We could say nothing about ourselves, our past or present situation. After this speech, we were each assigned a number. My number, and thus name, was 603.

We were then taken to a huge windowless cellar where we were ordered to undress. We were afraid that we would be led to the gas chambers, but, instead, we were told to parade in front of the S.S. men. They looked us over to check for diseases. Although we were naked, many of us still wore our shoes. We knew we would not be able to retrieve them if we took them off. The real reason I hadn't removed mine was that I had hidden a little photograph of my parents in one of them.

When the inspection ended, we were taken to the showers.

The shower room was huge, and we smiled with relief when the water proved to be real. Clean, striped dresses were then given to us by Polish inmates. We learned that they had been in the camp for some time, along with Russian prisoners of war. My shoes had gotten very wet, and my first thought as I took them off was to examine the little photograph to be sure it was all right. It was in pieces! I was heart-broken. The picture had meant so much to me and my sister Tobcia. We often looked at it to remind us of our beloved family. The photograph had embodied my prayer, my plea to my parents — wherever they were — to help us. I knew they were watching over us and I had faith in them.

Leipzig lager was more solidly constructed than the work camp in Hasak, but life was harsher there. Early each morning we were given our daily allowance of food: one slice of bread, a cup of black coffee and a small portion of watery soup. It wasn't nearly enough for the long day of work ahead.

The barracks themselves were all long, each holding about fifty women. Some barracks had three or four levels to their beds, but I was fortunate to be in one with only two-level bunk beds. Each bed was shared by two inmates and was made of four wooden poles which held up wooden pallets covered with a bit of damp straw. We were also lucky enough to be issued army blankets.

The Polish and Russian POWs were treated better. They held jobs in the kitchen or the hospital ward. In each of the barracks there were two Polish POW women to watch over us. They received packages of food from time to time from the Red Cross, so they always managed to look relatively presentable. They acted superior to us and had the right to report anything to the S.S.

The S.S. were female civilians dressed in military uniform; members of the Nazi movement, they were given full authority in the camp. We had an oberfuhrer, as well, who was the overall supervisor of the camp. He came twice a day, in the morning and after work, to make us stand on apel outside. It took approximately one hour to be counted, regardless of any inclement weather.

As in Hasak, the key to survival in Leipzig was to avoid getting sick. Any type of infection would have no hope of being cured. Even a bad cold endangered other inmates and oneself. We all suffered several illnesses at one time or another, but we tried hard not to let it show at work.

Our meisters were all German. They were elderly men who were too old to serve in the Army. They supervised and maintained the machines which we operated, and we were only allowed to speak to them at times when the machines needed repair. Any other conversations with these Germans was a punishable offence.

And so the same old struggle, the game of our life, continued in this new setting under even more hazardous conditions. In Leipzig, we never knew what to expect or who would be the next victim of a random act of sadism.

Autumn arrived bringing rain and cold winds. Wearing only my prison dress, with nothing underneath, I had no protection from the biting wind. We all looked the same in our one-size dresses.

Soon the winter of 1945 piled up high snow while the temperature in the barracks plummeted. After receiving our portions of bread, we ripped off pieces and stuffed them into our mouths like animals. Our block elster would then order us to keep quiet. A polish woman, we never asked her why she was in the camp. She was very rough and never looked straight at us. Even though we were from the same country, her attitude toward us was bitter.

We were kept so busy at work that we didn't have time to think about our gnawing hunger. My machine was complicated enough to keep my mind occupied.

My German meister wore civilian clothes. He was an older man, who constantly watched our work. When the lunch bell finally rang, we were allowed a brief opportunity to meet other inmates and share news of the outside world. There were rumors that Poland had been occupied by the Russians. Supposedly, English and American troops were already engaged in fighting on German soil. It seemed to me like a fairy tale.

XV

Pregnant Final Days

In Leipzig I made one close friend, Mrs. Herzburg, who had also come from the Hasak camp. Anna, or Mrs. Herzburg, was a sincere woman who treated me kindly. She had known my sister from her hometown, and we soon became close friends. We decided to share a bunk, Anna on the bottom and my sister and me on top. Although Mrs. Herzburg was very concerned with keeping clean, she was too large to comfortably make the climb to the higher bunk.

We learned that Anna's husband had been transported from Skarzysko to Buchenwald, but she hardly ever spoke of him or of anyone in her family. She always spent any free time lying on her bunk, her hands under her head, and her blue eyes staring blankly ahead.

When I climbed up or down, Mrs. Herzburg never seemed to notice the shaky disturbance, and she grew even more withdrawn as the months passed. She seemed too restless to do the work she was assigned. She grew pale and had a sad look about her. When I spoke to her, she seemed to be miles away.

In Leipzig, Anna had only a handful of married women to share her problems with. Most of us were young, single girls who had never experienced the loss of a husband or child. Just as I pitied my own sister, Tobcia, I also empathized with Mrs. Herzburg. Fortunately, my sister was one person Anna felt she could talk to. Tobcia and Anna had much in common, as they were both about the same age and had both known great happiness before the war had interrupted their marriages. I often found them whispering together, but it had never occurred to me that Mrs. Herzburg could be walking around with such an overwhelming secret. Anna was pregnant, and the secret soon spread through the camp like a dreaded disease.

Anna's body rounded out. Her eyes took on a wild, disturbed look. After work, she could hardly wait to get into her bunk and lie still.

We managed to get some news from other inmates, mostly rumors about the war soon ending. I often tried to lift Anna's spirits with these reports, but she was too preoccupied to care. Poor Anna knew she didn't have a chance. She had come from Skarzysko a pregnant woman and had known all along what awaited her.

Mrs. Herzburg's secret was safe for nearly six months. When the rumors reached the ears of the authorities, our block elster became wild. She ordered us out into the yard swearing revenge on the woman who was hiding this secret.

When we were all on apel, our block elster ordered any women who had become pregnant to step forward. We all stood frozen like corpses. Nobody said a thing. After a while, the S.S. guard angrily shouted that there would be an examination and the pregnant one would be punished by death.

That Sunday the barracks was surrounded by S.S. women who terrorized us with whips and marched us to the sick ward. We all had to undress and lie down on our backs while the Russian prison doctor touched our stomachs. The S.S. women stood over us throughout the examination.

Mrs. Herzburg was next to me. Her lips were white, her face a ghastly pale and her belly looked swollen. It was only then that I learned the awful truth.

The Russian doctor announced that Anna was the one, and the guard, brandishing her whip, ordered her victim to stand. Mrs. Herzburg crossed her arms over her stomach and then, by some miracle, the guard placed her whip back into her boot. She then screamed at Anna, "Do you understand what is waiting for you?"

Anna shook her head yes.

"In a short time, you whore," the guard continued, "you will be sent to Ravensbruck or Auschwitz."

When Anna realized that she was not going to be whipped or executed on the stop, her shoulders began to tremble. She dropped her head into her hands and sobbed. Even though she had been sentenced to death, we were all relieved that we would not have to witness it. We had become accustomed to instant killings before our eyes.

A woman from Krakow was also found to be pregnant. She and Anna were given patches to wear on their prison dresses. The patches identified them as traitors. Many of us felt anger towards their husbands who participated in the crime of begetting children. Now these unfortunate women had to face their punishment alone.

In the weeks before our freedom, the war remained in full swing. Hope was the bittersweet medicine which gave us the strength to go on living. Anna constantly wept tears of anger and exhaustion, as she waited to be sent away to the crematorium. She walked around like a living ghost, sometimes scavenging a little rotten food from the kitchen garbage.

Each time the sirens sounded, Anna would start to shake like a wounded animal. Finally, she was dismissed from work. Next morning when we heard the block elster's whistle, Mrs. Herzburg was the first to rise. She couldn't sleep. She stood in the doorway as we left the barracks to go to work and she said good-bye to each of us. Seeing tears in her eyes, I hugged her and begged her not to cry.

"Have hope," I said. "We'll soon be liberated."

That afternoon when I returned from work I saw that Anna was still with us. I threw my arms around her, hugging and kissing her. She had survived one more day. Only God could save Anna and her unborn child.

A toothache, too, could mean a ticket to the crematorium. My cheek had swelled out and the pain in my tooth had become so intense that I could hardly hold my head up. I had no choice but to tell my block elster, who gave me a pass to the sick ward. It was a deadly place, but there was no alternative. At the ward, two Russian women who called themselves doctors were taking care of the sick inmates. One of them looked into my mouth and picked up a large, rusty pair of pliers.

"Open your mouth as wide as you can," she commanded.

"What are you going to do?" I asked her.

"What do you expect me to do?" she retorted.

Her heavy hand clamped onto my face, while all at once she started to yank at one of my back teeth. I screamed like a mad man, the pain was so intense. Blood and pus oozed from my mouth. She gave me a piece of thick brown paper, stiff as cardboard, and told me to pack my mouth with it.

Meanwhile, liberation seemed more and more certain. My German meister started to ask me questions, but I was afraid to trust him. He could hardly look me in the eye, but he needed to talk about the German treatment of the Jews.

Selections were constantly made, and many were shipped off from Leipzig to Ravensbruck or Auschwitz in the last weeks. Knowing that liberation was so close gave us an especially sad feeling for those sent away.

Often during work, we would hear the siren and run to the shelter. Leipzig was being destroyed. We could feel the impact and hear the eerie whistle of the falling bombs. We spent more and more time in the shelters. Each time the siren sounded, my sister and I looked at each other, smiling with satisfaction over the crumbling of our cruel oppressor's empire. I feared nothing as much as not being able to take revenge on our enemy. I would only be satisfied upon seeing the Nazis humiliated while we walked free.

One day Anna and the other pregnant woman were assigned to Ravensbruck, along with all the inmates from the sick ward. I could not believe that we would never see Anna again. I couldn't bring myself to say goodbye to her that morning. Instead, I touched my fingers to her lips and turned away before she could see the tears in my eyes.

All day at the factory I was restless. Mrs. Herzburg had looked so heavy when we parted, being in her last months of pregnancy. I could hardly wait to return to camp that afternoon.

Perhaps a miracle would occur and Anna would still be there and not on line to the crematorium.

The sirens went off. Leipzig was once again under attack. The lights were flickering on and off making it impossible to work any longer. The S.S. hid in the bomb shelter, leaving us to fend for ourselves in the ammunition factory. When we returned to camp, we saw the place in disarray. The chaos was positively thrilling, but even more thrilling was the sight of Mrs. Herzburg waiting there for me and Tobcia. When she saw us, she threw her arms around us and started to cry hysterically. She told us that the transport of sick and pregnant women had been loaded onto a truck. When they were ready to pull out, though, the S.S. driver realized that the truck was overloaded. He glanced around and saw Anna with her big stomach.

"Step down!" he ordered. "You're too heavy. You will be deported in the next evacuation."

By now, the rest of the inmates had returned to the barracks and were all surrounding Anna. We clasped our hands and praised God that our friend had been saved. We whispered in her ear, "Don't you know? The Americans are coming!"

"We won't live to see it," Anna responded. In spite of our encouragement, she remained pessimistic. We couldn't lift her spirits.

The next April morning, the sun shone brightly. No Germans appeared to march us off to work. We were outside in front of the barracks when we saw the airplanes in the sky like a flock of silver birds. We knew they were on our side, but our dream of freedom still seemed too high to reach.

Suddenly the planes swooped down. The siren blared and everyone ran to the shelter beneath the barracks. Suddenly we heard an explosion; the barracks trembled. We were piled on top of each other with rubble falling from the ceiling. Somehow we all managed to leave the shelter in one piece.

Our block elster announced that we had caused all the trouble. When we were standing outside, the patrol planes had mistaken us for army troops and shelled our barracks.

But we were so desperate that we waved to them for help. One plane, flying low, dropped leaflets which read, "Be brave. You will be free soon."

We started to cry with all kinds of mixed feelings. Some inmates were happy; others were overwhelmed by sadness. My sister and I were crying hysterically.

"The end has come," she wailed. "Why couldn't our family have lived to see this?" We comforted each other with the hope of finding some of our brothers after liberation. We prayed that Shmulek was also waiting to be freed.

The bombing raged on for two unbelievable weeks. Liberation was no longer a fantasy — even Anna could see that. I finally noticed a slight smile on her face. She was excited by a carrot found near the garbage. Our meager slice of bread and ladle of soup wasn't enough for her and her unborn child.

It was just a matter of days now, and we knew that hunger wouldn't kill us as long as we could look forward to freedom. Then we could tell the world the truth — the whole truth.

One night, the lagerfuhrer took us on a march with thousands of other women. Anna was left behind in the barracks with a few other inmates who were too sick to march. She was lying down in the sick ward, fully expecting to be shot, when my sister and I managed to sneak in to say our goodbyes. She embraced us both.

"Don't cry, Mrs. Herzburg," I said. "You have a good chance now. Have faith!" I waved to her as I left. "You will see the liberation. Have strength!" And off we marched.

It was not until two years later that I found out what had happened to Anna. I was living in Augsburg, Germany, and had received some clues to her whereabouts from conversations with other liberated Leipzig inmates. They told me she had been reunited with her husband. Living with them in Feldafing was their son, the first baby born after the American liberation.

In 1948, I went to Feldafing to visit Anna, going first to the D.P. (Displaced Person) camp to obtain her whereabouts. I went directly to the address given to me.

She was living in a simple one-room apartment, but she seemed happy. She sat smiling, watching her beautiful baby son playing. I stood there waiting to see how she would greet me after all this time.

It took her a moment to recognize me. Then she stretched out her hand and let out a loud, happy scream. She was thrilled to see me and at last to share the good and the sad news of all our friends.

Years later, in America, I learned from the *New York Times* that Mrs. Herzburg's son had his bar mitzvah in New York. I looked her up and we spoke a few times. Anna passed away in her forties, but her son went on to achieve prominence.

XVI

Beware the Blessed Liberators

Our first day of freedom was a Sunday in May of 1945. After a cold rain, the sun came out, bright and warm. Even with the end in sight, the German sadism dictated a harrowing death march. We could see the flames of the American planes lighting up the dark sky like a messianic signal.

The oberfuhrer had ordered our immediate evacuation — but we were given no destination. We feared the worst. There was talk of escape, but everyone knew it was useless.

I was in the first block which began the march that evening. We were given two slices of bread for the trip. The S.S. guards kicked and shouted. Many were riding motorcycles, brandishing whips. We were like walking skeletons, passing abandoned ghost towns.

After a few hours, we rested in a field. At night we clung together on the wet ground, waiting for morning and the resumption of our march to hell or heaven.

We were exhausted. Inmates of every nationality were lying stretched out with their faces in the mud. We felt a mixture of pity and envy. I was ready to join them in eternal sleep, but my sister held me up by my arms. She kept saying, "Just another few hours and we'll reach our destination." I was sick with hunger. I wanted to vomit, but my stomach was empty. For days we sleepwalked without food or water. Those who couldn't go on just collapsed. There was no time or emotion left to fuss about these stiffened corpses, al-

though each could be someone's sister or mother. The herd
was driven on without even a backwards glance.

With our heads hung down and our bodies bent from
walking, we kept on for ten days. Then came a terrible wind,
bringing rain. It was a Saturday. Somehow, in the storm, a
small group of us became separated from the rest. We were
overjoyed to be on our own, but still we had to avoid the
machine guns of the S.S. With the rain and wind buffeting
us heavily, we looked for shelter.

Finally we came to a small house behind a large, horse-
drawn covered wagon. We knocked on the door, but a
woman wielding a broom warned us to stay away. With
nowhere to go, we hid in the wagon.

Night was approaching, and the war seemed no closer to
an end. The sky was aflame and the staccato shooting
seemed to go on forever. It was a long night sitting in that
wagon in our soaked prison dresses, shivering, dizzy from
hunger. Every minute we feared that the wagon would be
hit by an artillery shell.

Then we heard a noise close by. We looked out and saw
a soldier digging a trench. My sister whispered, "Listen, girls,
he's a Russian soldier." The relief was indescribable. My
sister walked over to the soldier who recognized our
uniforms.

"Yes," he said. "I am Russian. I see you were prisoners.
Well, now you are free."

We were directed by the Russian military to a Red Cross
station where we would be helped. The streets were littered
with dead horses, overturned wagons and dead and
wounded soldiers.

Finally we saw the Red Cross flag waving. We were surrounded by a babble of unknown languages. There were

thousands of other refugees like us who were given beds, a light meal and a medical examination. There were rumors that the Germans were regrouping for a counteroffensive, but our feet were too swollen to walk. We were soon the only two Jewish girls left among the prisoners.

The Germans did not surrender easily. They continued to murder innocent victims until the bitter end. The Russians encouraged us to help ourselves to any food and clothing we could find in the many abandoned houses. Tobcia and I scavenged in basements and closets to get dresses, shoes, and other belongings. We soon began to look like women again, but we still felt like prisoners.

We were less than strangers or refugees in Germany and we were desperate to get back to Poland. Perhaps there we would find relatives. But finding our way home was difficult. For weeks we struggled, mostly by foot, hitch-hiking when we could.

We started out on the road, the Russian military passing by in full force. The soldiers were all covered with dust, and many were wounded. They waved to us, some smiling, others sad. We walked all day until we reached a big house flying a red flag. Russian security guards were standing on either side of the door. We were happy to find what appeared to be a safe place.

We didn't tell the guards that we were Jewish. The officer in charge interrogated us. Finally, he told us we could stay with two Russian girls upstairs.

We were grateful to rest in peace for the night. We discovered that the two girls had also been prisoners at the Leipzig concentration camp. They knew we were Jewish, but were friendly, nevertheless.

There were two double beds in which all four of us slept comfortably. The next morning the girls made us hot tea and bread and jam. What a holiday! My sister wasn't too happy with the place, but as we needed our rest, she agreed to stay one more night.

We were going to sleep early when we heard two soldiers coming up the stairs to our room. At first I didn't pay much attention, since I thought they were coming to see the Russian girls. When the girls were questioned, they told them that we were Jewish. The soldiers then roughly ordered us to get dressed in five minutes. When I asked the girls what was going on, they just smiled and told us to have some fun.

I started to scream and pull my hair. One of the Russians struck me with his gun. We panicked and couldn't find our clothes in the dark. We ran down to the security officer and begged him to have pity on us. I screamed that it would have been better to have been killed by the Nazis. The officer ordered the soldiers to leave us alone and told us to go back upstairs. He apologized and promised that we would be protected, but we had already lost confidence in the Russians.

My heart was pounding, but we had no choice but to wait for morning before leaving. It was a shock to be struggling for survival so soon after liberation. Suddenly, the tall officer who had initially questioned us approached with his rifle on his shoulder. A shiver went through my body. He commanded the Russian girls to leave the bed. When I asked the girls why, they told me that the soldier wanted to make love to me and that I should give myself gladly because he had saved me. But he added that I would be raped by many more men before they went off to the front. They didn't care who the girls were or what condition they were in.

I pleaded with him. My sister also begged. But he paid no attention. He told us to be quiet and started to take off his uniform. I cried and screamed and scratched and kicked with all my strength. My struggle only aroused his lust, but it probably saved my life. Suddenly he got up, straightened his uniform and left.

The night that followed was long and scary, but when morning came, my sister and I picked ourselves up and started walking, never again to mention the ugly incident.

We had run out of words. Tobcia and I were lost in thought. The road seemed endless. We were depressed and exhausted. My heart pounded each time I started to think about the horrifying experience with the Russian soldiers. My body ached, and I could hardly walk. The pains persisted but my sister convinced me to be strong. She comforted me by telling me that we were lucky to escape a brutal gang rape. The physical pains would heal in time.

While walking, we searched the faces we passed, hoping to find someone we knew. We hoped to join other survivors to travel more safely together. Finally we stopped Fela, Dora, and Sara - three girls who had been with us in Leipzig. There was a warm reunion, and then without thinking, we found ourselves walking in a line, marching in rhythm, just as we had marched for the past three years.

We finally stopped in a lively town, full of elderly Germans, and, as everywhere else, the Russian military.

We put aside our fears and asked a Russian officer where we could stay. He told us which houses were abandoned and we chose a comfortable little farm house close to the road. Looking out the window, we could see the Russian army passing by. Marching along under Russian guard were captured German prisoners of war, many of whom were wounded. We took great satisfaction in seeing Nazi uniforms on the other side of suffering.

Sometimes I walked over and spit in their faces or called them bloody Nazi murderers and let them know how happy I was to witness their pain. I wanted to kill them, but my Jewish upbringing taught me that it would be up to God to punish these monsters.

Some of the Nazis tried to apologize saying it was the Fuhrer Hitler who brought war to his people. They said they were just following orders.

On our second night, we were awakened by loud noises. Armored cars and tanks were passing by. Suddenly we heard someone breaking through the door. We were immediately on our feet and dressed, as some Russian soldiers entered, led by a general.

After busying themselves with a map for a couple of hours, the officers remembered the five girls they saw and decided to have some fun. Again our struggle started, but this time we didn't panic. Having a general in the house gave us protection.

As the night went on the officers never seemed to tire of the game. They constantly forced themselves on us. My sister courageously called on the General for help, but he paid no attention to us. He self-righteously told my sister that there was a war going on and his officers didn't know whether or not they would ever see their homes again.

"But, General," my sister pleaded, "We are Polish girls, liberated after years of suffering under the Germans. I am sure you have heard what we went through."

"Yes," he said, "But we have also had our share of suffering."

We all stuck together, and although the officers continued to struggle with us, it was to no end. Ultimately, we managed to fight off the advances of the Russian army.

When morning arrived, we were happy to gain the relative safety of the road. After this second experience with the Russians, we developed an even deeper distrust of them. And we had so eagerly awaited the day that their red flag of freedom would wave! We thought the Russians were our friends, neighbors whom we could trust.

We pushed on for hundreds of miles with little food, not even knowing how far we had to go before reaching Poland.

At last, after six weeks on the road, we finally came to our last stop in Germany. Late in the evening we came upon a large, empty farmhouse. The master bedroom had two beds with high headboards, lots of pillows and soft down quilts. It looked like it was out of a picture book. We were dazzled by the wealth the rich Nazis had left behind before escaping to the American side. We even found thousands of marks — but they were worthless. The real find was the supply of food hidden in the basement. There were potatoes, carrots and cabbage. Knowing that we would not have to go hungry gave us an unfamiliar sense of security.

Tired from our trip, we went right to sleep on delightful feather beds that were so different from our three-tier wooden bunks. Wakened by the sun, we prepared anxiously for our homecoming to Poland.

My sister Tobcia discovered a train that would take us to Poland. What a relief to be finished with tramping along on the open road. That evening in the house we retrieved some songs from our youth and even dared to talk about our

future plans. After a thunderstorm we heard a rattling that
we hoped was caused by the wind. I was convinced that
someone was trying to get in.

We went downstairs to see what was causing the racket,
and our eyes were blinded by beams of light. Two Russian
soldiers with flashlights commanded us to get dressed. One
of them was a Mongol with slanted eyes and a short, wide
nose.

My friends were on the verge of collapse. Sara started to
scream like a little girl. My sister Tobcia begged the Russian-
speaking soldier for mercy, telling him the details of our
wartime ordeal. He apologized, but said he was ordered by
his superiors to round up all women. As there were no
German women left in town, we would have to serve as
victims.

Instead of panicking, I noticed something about the
Russian's features. While the Mongol was hitting us with his
rifle and pulling and shoving us around I whispered to
Tobcia my suspicion that the other soldier was Jewish. Over-
hearing, the Russian soldier seemed stunned. He pulled
back his rifle and demanded that I repeat what I'd just said.

I spoke to him directly in Yiddish: "I suspect that you are
also Jewish."

He reddened and immediately ordered his companion
to stop pushing us out the door. He stood bewildered until
the words could come out. "What a miracle to find Jewish
girls!" he gushed in Yiddish. "I thought I'd never see Polish
Jewish survivors this far west."

He told us that he was a Polish Jew who had left his family
to escape the Nazis. He ended up joining the Russian army.
His only hope was to survive the war and locate his family.
He cried, embraced us and called us his sisters. He warned

the Mongol not to mention the incident to anyone, and before departing, he said, "Thanks to Rachela and mama loschen you have all been spared."

The next day we were ready to make our way to Poland, our faith in human decency partially restored. The German railway station was demolished, but a Russian officer directed us to take any eastbound train. No tickets would be necessary.

"But what city should we stop at?" I asked the officer.

He looked at me and asked, "Don't you know your own home town?"

"Yes," I answered and almost choked, "but we have no home anymore. We have no place to go." With that he realized that we were Jewish survivors, and recommended that we make Lodz our first stop. At least in such a big city we would find many of our own kind.

The trip to Poland took several days. As we sat in the open car, twirling trees and little farm children waved goodbye to us. "Good riddance to you," I thought, anxious to soon break away from this large European graveyard.

XVII

Coming Home

The war was over. but black smoke still poured from the wreck or our lives. The railway east took us back in time to our neighbors, friends, and beloved families.

It was late in the evening when we reached Lodz. The station was packed. We stood on the platform like lost sheep until a well-groomed man approached us and asked who we were. We replied proudly, "We are Jewish survivors." He said he was from the Jewish committee which had been established by and for survivors. He would help us find shelter at the committee's headquarters.

On the way, I noticed that the houses in Lodz were intact and the streets of Lodz were lively, unbelievably normal.

The Jewish committee greeted us warmly. The place was packed with survivors hoping to find information. My desire to hear a word about family and friends was stronger than my fatigue, and I too found myself asking questions. My brother Shmulek was the only one I could reasonably expect to ever see again. So I searched for survivors of Buchenwald who might have known him.

After hours of waiting, we were assigned a room on the fifth floor of a nearby building. The room had only a few mattresses, a little table and two chairs. The five of us had to share these close quarters, but we weren't fussy. We were given some food and a little pocket money to help us get by. Tobcia wanted to return to her home to recover the goods she and her husband had left with her neighbors. We all convinced her that it was too dangerous. Large cities, such as Lodz and Warsaw, were the only safe places for Jews.

We heard of many happy reunions, and I dreamed of falling into the arms of one of my brothers. But as time passed, it became more and more difficult to remain optimistic. One sunny day, I recognized a young man named Monek who had been with Shmulek at Hasak lager, and had been good friends with Joshua.

"Yes, Rachela, I have seen your brother Shmulek," he said. "He is in Feldafing and doing fine." I gave a scream of happiness. My first thought was that my father's wish had come true. Someone had survived to say Kaddish for him. Tears of joy rolled down my face. Monek hesitated, then finally told me the sad news. Joshua died on his lap the day before liberation following a two-week march.

My sister was so happy to hear about Shmulek and tried to ease my pain about Joshua. "After all, my dear," she said, "you weren't married to him, not even engaged. He was a friend." But Joshua stayed in my mind. How pitiful! He had lost his chance for freedom just one day before liberation. It was my love for him that had kept me alive through the worst times, and it was very difficult now for me to accept his death.

As survivors registered at agencies all across Poland, the numbers began to roll in. We soon learned that three million Polish Jews had perished. I can understand how such a number, to some, must have been impossible to believe. But we were there. We had seen it. As horrifying as the death toll was, it helped to know that so many others had experienced the same devastation. Had I been the only one to have lost my home and family, I would have surely gone mad.

One by one, our roommates were finding partners, getting married and moving out. Most of them eventually emigrated to Israel. One of the girls wound up in South America, joining family that had gone there before the war. I was determined that my sister Tobcia also build a new life for herself.

We were constant visitors to the Jewish Committee headquarters, hoping for news of my brother's arrival from Germany. As waves of new people came and went, some met only disappointment, while others gushed with smiles after finding a long-lost relative or friend. It was wonderful to watch their dreams link and take shape.

One day, a visitor, a man in a Russian uniform, looking very sad, seemed familiar to me.

"I know you from some place,"he said. "You are Rachela, aren't you?"

"Yes," I replied suddenly recognizing him. "And you are Joel."

"Yes," he said. Joel had been our closest neighbor back in Wonchok.

We joyfully embraced each other. He cried and kept saying, "My dear, finding you is finding a sister."

During the war. Joel had married Sara, my sister's best friend. Sara and Tobcia had attended school together and were as close as sisters. We were saddened to hear that his wife and six-month-old baby had been sent to the gas chambers. Joel survived by hiding out in the forest with a group of partisans.

At the end of the war, a wounded Joel was found by Russian soldiers who took him back to Russia. He was in a hospital for many weeks before he was well enough to return to Poland, where he learned that the rest of his family had perished. He was alone.

When I told Joel about Tobcia, his sorrowful face changed. He was excited to hear that she, too, had survived. I asked him to come home with me, and he was pleased to accept my invitation. Tobcia was stunned and thrilled to see him.

Joel soon became a constant visitor. I considered him to be a big brother and hoped that he might become my brother-in-law.

Early one morning, I heard a knock at my door. I hesitated to open it, since my sister and Dora had gone shopping. As it turned out, my visitor was a handsome young man with a pleasant smile. He introduced himself as Heniek, our roommate's cousin, who had come to find his family.

He had survived the horrors of several camps, Buchenwald included. Despite everything, he remained optimistic and kind-hearted. When he spoke to me, his face would shine. He visited me often, and within a short while we realized that we were suited for each other. It was all so confusing. Though still young in years, it seemed as if my youth had been stolen from me. The girl in me yearned for romance, yet the woman in me was afraid to reach for any happiness. My sister, fond of Herb, encouraged me. We were delighted to learn that Herb, then called Heniek, wasn't alone. One of his brothers, as well as an aunt and an uncle, had also survived the war.

In November of 1945, Tobcia married Joel. I invited Herb to the wedding, which was held in our one-room apartment. Just a few guests were present, and I could not help thinking back to her gala first marriage. How different everything was. I remembered how we had carried on when we discovered that the wedding food was missing. Now our parents were missing, as were our brothers, sisters, uncles, aunts, cousins and friends.

Though the happiness of the moment was tinged with sadness, we did what we could to celebrate. Herb decided to propose to me at the wedding. I thought it was too soon, but Herb was positive that I was the right girl for him. He gently shared his plans for us in words that were simple and wise.

Holding my hand against his heart, he said, "My dear Rachela, I will not promise you health or riches, because such things can only be left in God's hands. But I promise to love you. I will love you as long as we're together."

My teenage brother was still on my mind. I decided I would not get married until I could bring Shmulek home.

The borders were opened and Tobcia made arrangements for me to travel to Germany in search of Shmulek. It took days, but a group of us finally reached the refugee camp in Feldafing, Germany.

The camp looked too much like a concentration camp. My companion Moshe was familiar with the place, and he took me past the guard to the administrator's office.

I told him my reason for coming to Feldafing, and I could see that he was taken aback.

"Is something wrong?" I asked. "Is my brother okay?"

"Yes," he said, "But, Miss Walshaw, your brother just left yesterday for England with a group of youngsters. The English Jewish community sponsored these youngsters, and your brother was among them." And I had come so far! I couldn't believe it!

I had missed Shmulek by one day. Then the administrator took out a picture of my brother to assure me that he was okay. Holding the picture in my hand, I broke down.

"Don't cry, my dear," the man said to me. "Be happy that your brother is alive. You will see — you will have much pleasure from him. He is in England, in a free country, where he will have lots of opportunities."

After resting for a few days, I joined a group going back to Poland. Within a few days, I was back in the arms of Tobcia and Joel, who were delighted to hear that Shmulek was safe.

Meanwhile, we were once again on the move. Tobcia and Joel wanted to try their luck in Wroclaw, a city that had been returned to Poland after the war. Many survivors were resettled there. We were given a well-furnished apartment that had apparently belonged to the S.S. As the city was only recently liberated, there were not many Poles living there yet. There were mostly Russians and Germans.

Joel began trading on the black market. This was illegal and risky, but it enabled us to get by. Herb was also living in Wroclaw, along with his brother. When he heard that I had returned from Feldafing and was living in Wroclaw, he immediately came to join me.

Shortly thereafter, my sister made arrangements for my wedding. Held on January 2, 1946, the brief ceremony was attended by a rabbi and a few friends. Tobcia baked a sponge cake and cookies, and we got some wine and beer. I wore a simple, everyday dress. Tobcia gave me a white kerchief to cover my head, but I felt like wearing a black one. Even on this day of joy I mourned my losses.

A Jewish organization in England supplied me with Shmulek's address. I wrote to him, and we began a correspondence.

XVIII

Shmulek's Survival

While Tobcia and I had been on our way to the work camp in Leipzig, Shmulek was enduring his own harrowing journey.

First, he was forced to help load the old camp's heavy machinery onto trains bound for Germany. Then he and the other male inmates were shipped off to Buchenwald. This was part of Germany's effort to cover up the Holocaust before the Russians marched in to Poland.

At Buchenwald the men were ordered to undress and shower. Selections eliminated those Jews not fit for more slave labor. Those with remaining strength to exploit were assigned an identifying number. Shmulek's was 67832. He fully expected to be killed, but instead was moved to Szliben, near Leipzig, with about two thousand others. It was cold, and some of the inmates were forced to build their own barracks.

Shmulek was assigned to laying railway lines. This was a good job for him as the bigger fellows did most of the hard work. Also, the German railway supervisor took a liking to him, supplying him with extra rations as well as news from the front.

One night, the camp was nearly destroyed by an explosion in the ammunition factory. Shmulek survived to be sent to Flosenberg, where a new ammunition factory was being built. His German supervisor warned him not to go, as the work and conditions were worse than in Buchenwald.

Shmulek, however, wanted to stay with his friend, Hofen-
bach, who had been with him in Camp Hasak. The German
had been right. Flisberg was murderous. Plucky Shmulek
was able to pick up some cigarettes from an Italian POW,
and with these cigarettes he bought his way onto a transport
of sick people headed back to Buchenwald.

This was already the beginning of 1945, and the inmates
knew that the American army was nearby. They could hear
sporadic shooting and were sustained by hopes of liberation.

One day the Germans evacuated all the Jews. Shmulek
pretended to be Polish and survived once more. Soon
afterwards all the Poles were loaded unto sealed box cars
bound for Veinmark. Many died during the trip. The
remaining prisoners were regrouped until finally two S.S.
with automatic weapons simply opened fire on them as they
stood in the cars.

Shmulek was hit. But, miraculously, he awoke the next
morning in a moving car full of bloody bodies. Most were
dead, but he could hear the faint moans of the few who were
only wounded like himself. He pulled himself free of the
heavy bodies and saw that he had been shot in the leg. He
could hardly stand, but, with all his strength, he hauled five
other survivors out of the pile.

When the train stopped, the doors opened and the
survivors were ordered to dig a huge ditch. A fire was started
in the hole where they were told to throw the corpses. The
wounded were pushed in on top of them. Shmulek put on
a convincing act that he was fine, and he once again survived. This led him to Dachau, where by pretending to be
Polish, he received medical treatment that included an
operation without anesthetic.

Rumors were circulating that the Germans had mined the whole camp. Lying in the hospital, Shmulek forced himself to sleep so that he would not be conscious when they were all blown up.

But they were not blown up. After a full night's sleep, Shmulek woke to see Black soldiers wearing strange uniforms and speaking a strange language. They were Americans. Shmulek had lived to see liberation.

By then, however, the condition of his leg had worsened. Gangrene had set in, and the American doctor who examined it suggested amputating it. Shmulek refused. After having endured so much pain, he could not face life as a cripple.

The doctor was too busy to argue, so Shmulek was left to his own resourcefulness. An American nurse took pity on him and brought the doctor back for an immersion technique which would draw out the infection. It took a while and was very painful, but the therapy eventually worked. The doctor was so proud of his medical miracle that he had a photograph taken of himself, Shmulek, and the nurse.

Shmulek survived by his own wits. I yearned to see my brave little brother and wrote to him faithfully until the day we were finally reunited.

XIX

New Beginnings

Five generations of my family lay buried in Polish soil, but there was no longer anything to keep me there. We owned nothing. Our home and community, our roots, our nationality — everything was gone.

There was only my family — at least, what was left of it. My husband and I were very close to Tobcia and Joel. We lived together and planned a future together far away from the European house of horrors.

With the borders then closed between Poland and Germany, illegal crossing was precarious. The only free zone was in American-occupied Germany. There we could find true protection. We contacted a group from the Bricha organization who guided survivors from Eastern Europe and smuggled them to Israel or the West.

Even though I wanted to leave, I was not up to travelling again so soon after the ordeal of the past three years. I was often dizzy and nauseous and without an appetite. All I wanted to do was sleep. Herb was concerned when I started losing weight. I finally decided to see a doctor, and that's when I learned that I was pregnant.

My mind was racing. We were survivors on the road. The only support and stability I had were Heniek's devotion and love. He was happy that I was pregnant and constantly told me not to worry. We lived with the hope that our first child would know only health and happiness.

We left in July, 1946, on an evening when bright stars shone in the sky. We put ourselves in the hands of the people from Bricha, positive that it was our last chance to escape the claws of the Russian bear. Bricha agents prepared us for the final move and instructed us on how to steal across the border. We committed every word to memory.

Midnight was the appointed hour when the Russian guards would hopefully be sound asleep. My last good-bye to Poland was in total darkness. We walked in single file beneath the silent stars.

High mountains stood between us and freedom. The road was studded with treacherous boulders. After walking a while, I began to feel short of breath. My feet felt numb. I stopped; I couldn't go on. I felt faint as if I had been drugged. I heard dogs barking as we approached the boarder. Everyone was whispering in excitement. After hours of sweating and battling exhaustion, we had finally reached our goal. It was early in the morning — the grass still wet with dew — when we allowed ourselves a break on the free soil of Czechoslovakia. It felt good to rest for a couple of hours, but we had to force ourselves on. We had to reach the Czech city of Bratislava before we could consider ourselves safe.

Once there, we rested for five days in an army barracks. These barracks reminded me of the concentration camp, but we were free and the guards were there to protect not torture us.

We travelled through many cities before we reached Augsburg, Germany, in August of 1946, and this is where we made our temporary home. This was where Herb's brother, Haim, his aunt and uncle, and their son Harvey, all survivors, had settled five months ago. We first located the

Jewish Committee of Augsburg, who found us a little furnished apartment close to Tobcia and Joel. Our one-bedroom apartment had been owned by Jews before the war, as were all the homes distributed to "displaced persons" like us. Only a handful of the original Jewish Augsburgers were able to trickle back to their homes after the war.

We were heartened to see that the local synagogue, like the rest of this clean city, was intact. While Augsburg was nice enough, the American rations were limited and fresh food virtually non-existent. There were about twenty other survivor families, so we had some feeling of security and community. The crowds of clean-cut American G.I.'s were so much more civilized than their Russian counterparts.

The Germans citizens, their human and financial resources devastated by the war, tried hard to make amends. We heard over and over again how it was not their fault — the war, the invasions, the extermination of the Jews. None if it was their fault. I would look at their faces, and their pleading eyes would almost win my sympathy, but I could not shake the vision of blood dripping from their hands.

My sister's apartment was nearby, and we were together all the time. Tobcia and Joel had a son Solomon, named after our father. By then we had given up hope of finding other relatives. We were the world to each other. Our little apartment gave me the security and sense of humanity I needed in my later months of pregnancy.

Tobcia and Joel decided to be the pioneers. I desperately wanted to be with them, but Tobcia insisted we stay behind and wait to hear from them. When we finally received word from them, they told us under no circumstances should we think about going to the new state of Israel. It was 1948 and existence as still very uncertain in the infant Jewish state. We were heartbroken, but what could we do?

In December of that year, Shmulek surprised us by visiting us in Augsburg. It was a great thrill to see my brother again. Shmulek had changed so much in the three years we had been separated. Ravaged by wartime experience, the former young boy was now a grown up young man dressed in modern English style. I didn't know which tears were joy and which were sorrow, but at last we were reunited. I was thankful to God that my father had a surviving son to say Kaddish for him and that Shmulek was thriving in his adopted country.

Shmulek and I talked for hours about the past and our family who had perished for the world's madness. I could hardly bear saying goodbye to Shmulek who had his life in England awaiting him. All that awaited us was uncertainty.

With both Tobcia and Shmulek gone, it was a lonely wait, but we got to know our German neighbors a bit. We became friendly with the Schmidt family who helped us get fresh milk and vegetables, a rare commodity right after the war.

In time, we even opened up enough to talk about the war. The Schmidts' daughter, who was very bright and studying to be a nun, took special interest in my life story. After listening to me, she would well up with pity and start crying. She told her mother, who opposed her becoming a nun, how proud she was to be a true Christian — unlike the evil Nazis.

"Papa, she said, "our country will forever be marked with blood for what our Fuhrer brought upon our brothers and sisters."

I was impressed with young Miss Schmidt's sincerity, and I eventually heard the Schmidts' own dramatic story. Mr.

Schmidt had formerly been married to a Jewish woman who
bore him two sons. One day Mr. Schmidt came home from
his frequent travels to find his wife cheating on him with a
Jewish friend of theirs.

The enraged Mr. Schmidt divorced his wife and got
custody of the children. The current Mrs. Schmidt was a
lovely young woman who originally was the paid
housekeeper and guardian of the children. While the step-
mother became an accepted member of the family, Mr.
Schmidt allowed the boys' mother to visit while he was away.

With the outbreak of the war, Mr. Schmidt feared for his
sons' lives. They were raised Christian, but their Jewish
blood was their death warrant. The father made the difficult
decision of sending the boys to England with their mother.
During my many months with the Schmidts I saw the boys,
who had settled in Munich after the war, on several oc-
casions.

My own son was on the way to this world as a cold autumn
gave way to a snowy winter. In the middle of a snowstorm I
was hit with labor pains and had to be brought to the
hospital. It was January 5, 3:00 p.m., when my son Solomon
was delivered. I wished for my son a world of safety among
people he could trust. Our dream was to raise our child in
Palestine.

My sister Tobcia arranged a circumcision ceremony and
party in our one-bedroom apartment that was attended by
our small but intimate circle of survivor friends. Besides
Tobcia and Joel, our social world included Herb's brother
Haim and Mrs. Schmidt — all of whom helped take care of
our little Shloime.

Over the months ahead we were given the opportunity
to visit places like Munich, my Yiddish helping me to make

conversation in German. Wherever we met Germans we found most of them to be bitterly ashamed of their recent behavior. We, on the other hand, were beginning to slowly recover from the years of humiliation and fear. Our past truly took the back burner when, after three years of paper work and hope, the golden gates of America finally opened for us.

Our opportunity for freedom in the New World notwithstanding, I had my share of doubts. Along with the great news from the Joint Distribution Committee came the news that I was now pregnant with another child. It was exciting to think that our next child might be born in America, but what would we find in this new country whose language and customs were so foreign to us? How would we find a home, jobs, or friends?

Herb was enthusiastic and full of optimism for our successful transition and that of little Shloime, by then two years old. Besides, his brother Haim and his aunt and uncle had already left for the States and would be able to show us the ropes. It was on one of my trips back from the Committee for orientation about America that my accident occurred.

I was walking with Shloime down the incline that led to our apartment. I slipped on some lose rocks and took a bad fall. My son was crying to see his mother needing help from passers by to get back on her feet. I felt shaky, my heart beating with fear for the child I was carrying.

Recurrent backaches gave way to stomach pain until I realized that something serious had happened. I suddenly began to bleed profusely. I was all alone. During the unending torrent I lunged for the bed, calling out to our hard-of-hearing neighbor, Mr. Schmidt, for help. I felt sure that my life was flowing away from me. For at least a half hour I lay there with my senses reeling, my bleeding body in agony. I recall mewing like a cat until finally hearing Mr. Schmidt's voice at the door and his gasp, "Oh my God," when he discovered me.

I lay in the hospital for a full week, receiving daily blood transfusions. When I was allowed to return home to my husband and child I heard the whole story of how Mr. Schmidt, himself a sick man in his late sixties, ran as fast as he could to get help for me. Mr. Schmidt has long since passed on, but I shall always cherish his memory as one who saved my life. Despite many Germans and because of one of them, I was two times a survivor.

I was very fortunate to have survived the great loss of blood, and our American doctor assured me that I'd be able to have healthy babies in the future. That future in America had to be postponed for the months of my recuperation, but on December 14, 1949, we finally left German soil, drenched with red blood and black memories. On December 18, at 3:00 p.m., we joined twelve hundred fellow emigrants of various nationalities and religions in setting sail for America aboard the USAT *Gen. W. G. Haan.*

During our ten days at sea we concentrated on putting behind us all memories of death camps, forced labor camps, starvation, persecution, fear and humiliation. Our wake was tumultuous and churning; our prow cutting staunchly ahead. Departure from the land of memory would not be smooth sailing until we cleared the sea of self-pity and the reef of guilt.

I was a young girl of fifteen when the war began, a woman of twenty-five when I stepped off that ship. Perhaps with the help of this log I shall some day come to terms with the lost years of my life.

XX

Samuel's English Chronicles

I was liberated by the American army in May of 1945. When the war ended I was in Germany's Dachau concentration camp. A few weeks later some 500 child survivors like myself were transferred by the United Nations Repatriation Association to a kinderblock in Feldafing, Germany. During the war the same facility housed a training camp for the Hitler youth.

Everyone in our special group of young survivors had a hard time trying to take care of ourselves. We weren't skin and bones anymore, but I can't say we cherished all that powdered food. Our major preoccupation was concern about our lost families. I knew in my heart that my parents and most of my family must have perished. My homeland, my birthplace, was behind me now forever. My only hope was that some of my sisters might have survived, and that eventually we would be able to find each other. I made sure to register my name and photo with the community authorities. This way anyone searching for me would be able to track me down no matter where in the world I was to be resettled.

It was August 1945. The announcement came that the British government had agreed to absorb a number of the younger and healthier Eastern European survivors. They wanted a ratio of two boys for every girl. We took the opportunity with much enthusiasm since we were desperate to get out of Germany.

The long-awaited day of departure for England finally arrived in November of 1945. Three large bombers flew in to an airfield near Feldafing. These Royal Air Force Lancasters were still fitted out for combat. Approximately two hundred boys and girls were crowded into these giant birds that had no seats or windows and few facilities. The excitement revved up with the massive propellers, as this eventful and emotional flight took us from the land of death to a military airfield in the north of England. The R.A.F. fellows were very polite. For the first time since the war began we were treated like human beings. I got off the plane with mixed feelings, but the whole gang of us boys went a bit wild when we finally arrived in Britain. We didn't know how to act without overseers. The sight of bicycles and motorbikes at the airfield made us desperate for a little joy. We got hold of some bicycles and were riding around the airfield at breakneck speed. We made a mess of that airfield. We were two hundred animals, not boys. The R.A.F. was very understanding, though, realizing that we had been confined for the last several years.

We were soon called into a hanger where there were people from the U.N. ready to take us away to an absorption and training facility. They took a few score of us on a two-hour train ride to Wintershill Hall. I was very impressed at how well the Hall was prepared for our arrival. I remember our first meal. There were many incredible dishes, but the white bread was my favorite. The variety of food was stunning, but it was bread that we had dreamed about for years.

The facility was like a little mansion, completely independent and situated on its own grounds. It had everything, even table tennis and tennis courts. We stayed there about two months, the first order of business being to teach us English. We were also given a lot of free time and a choice of sports activities. Knowing what we went through, they exempted us from the usual British school regimentation.

Wintershill Hall was dominated by two groups who competed for our souls: Bnei Akiva and Hashomer Hatzair. The former wanted us to retain our religious identity and practice, while the latter was on the secular side. Even though our sentiments leaned to religious belief, our juvenile behavior often deteriorated to the downright rowdy. As much as the institution tried to give us a normal life and a routine, we couldn't seem to feel normal. We wanted to behave well and conform on one hand, but the urge to act out was irrepressible. Our psychological injuries were too deep, too recent, to allow us to maintain any decorum at Wintershill Hall.

We divided up into fairly rigid cliques. I stuck together with the boys I had met at the Feldafing Displaced Persons camp in Germany. The core group consisted of Charlie, Joe, Abish, Karl and myself, the whole gang extending to ten fellows.

One day we were offered a transfer to Manchester. I didn't know where Manchester was, but I was keen on moving around and seeing everything in England. About twenty-five of us were brought to a youth hostel on Northumberland Street in Manchester. Most of us were Polish, with a smattering of Hungarians.

We eventually acclimated ourselves, got to know the city and began to communicate more easily with the local British folk. At the hostel we were to continue learning, eventually find trades and move out. Teachers were brought in to teach us English and math, teaching us sixteen-year-olds what we normally would learn in the fifth grade. Our behavior gradually left the elementary school level, and we were almost mature enough to be teenagers.

As I slowly regained a sense of normalcy, I even regained some of the Hebrew education of my childhood. I was chosen by Mr. Pinchower, the headmaster, to be the gabbai, calling people up to the Torah and reading from it as well. I soon turned down the job because I was not observant enough to deserve it.

I was quite ambivalent about religion at the time, even though most of my friends in the hostel remained observant. My circumstances had given Judaism too many unpleasant associations. Even before the war Polish kids were always pulling on my sidecurls. Very soon, religion meant a stigma so treacherous that I had to fight for my life because I was born into a minority faith. There was no spiritual or communal richness to consider when all I felt at the time was the lonely horror of living on a planet where everyone hated me for being a Jew.

I tried to make a new identity for myself, but it's impossible to really stop being a Jew. The Yellow Star can never really come off. My youthful struggles with Jewish identity gradually gave way to proud identification and support of Israel. I still don't observe the full Jewish rituals that I knew as a child, but I now greatly respect those Jews — especially those survivors — who did remain consistently religious and observant. I was a rebel and not a follower in other respects as well, and poor Mr. Pinchower had his hands full with me. I was the strongminded ringleader, and even bribes didn't get me to fall in line. The gang and I took out our rage with many senseless acts of vandalism and petty theft. The police lost a lot of bicycles to the boys of Northumberland Street, but the authorities were very understanding and lenient when addressing our criminal binges.

We also fought quite a bit among ourselves. It was usually the Polish boys against the Hungarians. While food was life itself only months before, we had massive food fights that drove the frightened headmaster out to the streets for help. Even the police got pelted with vegetables and other ammunition when they were called in. We did calm down after several more months, realizing that the world could be a sane place after all, and that learning English and a trade could make a big difference in our lives.

I was in the English hostel for a while when I got jolted back to the world of my past and my family. My sisters had tracked me down through the refugee agencies. It was a great joy and relief to know that I was not alone. My cousin had also found me, and the very first letter that I had received was from him, signed Zysman Warszauer. Now this was the same name as my brother, and I couldn't understand how my brother could have written me when I knew he had perished. When I started to read the Polish, I realized that it was from my Warsaw cousin.

He has since died in Israel. He was exactly my age, but was not in the camps. He was the cousin who came bringing typhus which my sister and I contracted. His mother died soon after he returned to the Warsaw Ghetto. Zysman bravely escaped the ghetto and was a shepherd during the war for a Polish family. He owed his life to the fact that he was a blond little boy who did not look Jewish. After the war he packed a parcel and started walking during the nights. He managed to make his way from Poland all the way to Israel.

I was glad to make contact with cousin Zysman, but I couldn't wait to see my beloved sisters again. In 1948 I was able to get the special passes to travel in Germany and to visit my sisters in Augsburg. We had an emotional reunion. They wanted me to stay with them, and for all of us to make plans to move to Israel. But I didn't want to stay in Germany another day. I had made close friends in England who were like brothers to me.

I felt settled in England. While central Europe made me nervous, I found British non-Jews to be decent people. I have not encountered any anti-Semitism in England, and the Jewish community received me very well. With a new home to return to, I parted company with my sisters, maintaining close contact with them over the years.

Back at the hostel, I had to turn my attention to making a living. Most of the boys had started finding jobs and going out on their own. At first I thought I'd be a dentist. I was doing well in school, but I didn't have the patience to learn dentistry for so many years before being able to make a living. I wanted to earn money right away, and I wanted desperately to be independent. Too many fields seemed unsuitably boring to me.

By the time seventy percent of the boys were working, I was getting labeled as lazy. Mr. Pinchower found me a job in town making leather purses, where I would cut the purse design out with a press and then deliver the heavy pieces to the boss' house each day by bike. I earned thirty bob, but I wasn't learning anything about the trade. After two weeks of that drudgery I gave it up.

Our pocket money from the hostel was only half a crown. We were given second-hand clothes by Jewish benefactors, while the only jacket I owned was a brown Sabbath jacket that I quickly outgrew. Fortunately, women volunteers came to wash and mend our clothes. These kind women who gave us so much of their time were the only "mothers" we knew at this crucial time in our lives.

Our "father" figure, Mr. Pinchower, left the hostel and was replaced by a Mr. Amen from Belgium. He was only in his twenties, but he was quite capable. After all, he had the resourcefulness to escape the war and make his way to England.

Amen helped me with my reluctance to get tied down to a boring job, convincing me to learn any trade and then go out on my own when I was ready. He also politely reminded me that my allowance would be withheld if I didn't go out and look for work.

We talked about different professions that I might go into. Finally, Mr. Amen arranged to take me to his best friend, a furrier, to show me what this trade was all about. At the interview I met two brothers who were partners in the fur business. They were lovely people, fine human beings, and they were willing to take me on. They assured me that it was a profitable trade, and introduced me to the handcrafting side where I could start immediately. I was shown how to operate a few machines, and I quickly picked up the necessary skills.

I started off at twenty-seven shillings a week—fairly good for those days. In a few short years I was making and repairing elegant coats and capes. I earned enough to move out of the hostel and share a flat with a friend. After saving up a decent sum of money, I was determined to strike out for myself in the business world. I wanted full control of a business from the top down, rather than trying to slowly work my way up from the bottom.

When I investigated the retailing trends it appeared as though costume jewelry was in great demand and offered the best returns on investment. It was a risky business, but my second career in the jewelry trade grew into a success. At twenty-five I was truly happy with my life and financial independence. I was driving a Hillman Minx and living in my own flat on Corporation Street in Manchester. I would go into London on a weekly basis to purchase stock and spend some leisure hours dancing. It was about time, but this socially deprived fellow was finally feeling confidant enough to enjoy going out with girls.

Elaine was smart, sensible and fun to be with. When we first met I felt that she was meant for me. I was twenty-six at the time, and was sure that this young lady was about twenty-one. I arranged to ring her the next day for a sightseeing trip to Blackpool. Despite her poise, gorgeous figure and elegant dress, it turned out that she was only seventeen and living with her very dear mother. I regretfully explained that I was too old for her, but she would have none of it.

I couldn't stop going out with her, either. She was great company and a highly capable manager of a clothing shop. A few weeks later I asked her to work for my jewelry business on Corporation Street in Manchester. She accepted my offer and was soon my top sales girl. Instead of insisting on being taken to shows, she often worked hard and long hours to help us design a new line of jewelry.

After going out for four years we got engaged. We were ready for marriage, but wanted to buy a house first. We then bought a dilapidated house that Elaine and I did up oursel-ves with eighteen months of tearing down and building up. The old place looked beautiful when Elaine finally became a bride at age twenty-three. The ceremony was at Crumpsall Synagogue, Elaine's favorite. While we lived at 38 Cavendish Road, my wife continued working for the company. Our son Brenton was born in 1963. When I saw him in the hospital, I became a different person. I realized that I was a married man, a family man, and that I must give my son everything that I didn't have.

With my wife standing by me at every step, encouraging and helping me in every way, I have worked hard to provide financial security and a fine education for my sons Brenton, Darren and Jason, who should never know the barbed wire world of Eastern Europe. With ambition, market research and a little luck I began investing in different fields. I crossed over from the jewelry business to the handbag trade, designing a jeweled bag that proved to be popular. I anticipated the manufacturing boom in Hong Kong and Korea and also concentrated on plastics.

Today, I only maintain limited contact with my business affairs, leaving it all in the loyal and capable hands of my managers. I therefore have the opportunity to enjoy more leisure time, to savor my life and to appreciate the goals we have achieved. Our greatest joy is our three wonderfully devoted sons who live nearby. This close-knit, loving family is the greatest achievement that my wife and I have attained. We now put much of our energies into our synagogue and to philanthropic organizations like the 45 Aid Society.

When someone finds out that I lived through the Holocaust they often ask me if I think about it all the time. I can honestly say that I don't. People have short memories. The Holocaust is now like a big bad dream. Sometimes I return to that nightmare. When something goes wrong in business, I revert to my past and remember how my chief desire during the war was to have a piece of bread. It feels like a sin to complain now, and this perspective makes any setbacks seem easier. My past is like a safety valve for me. The older survivors think more about the Holocaust than I do. I was just young enough to tuck it away like a dream. When I need it, I can roll out the memories from under my bed. Otherwise, I've done well to have kept my past out of my daily life.

The Holocaust did not make us survivors ambitious. Either you were born ambitious, or you were not. Even in the camps I was ambitious. My ambition was not only to survive, but to do well for myself. I extend my ambition to my sons too. I gave them everything, and they are giving me plenty of naches (joyful satisfaction) in return.